U

UNBOXED

25 Women Share How To
Break Free & Soar

Volume One

For more information to obtain rights contact: or request interviews:

BTV Publishing and Consulting
3451 Washington Avenue, Suite B
Gulfport, MS 39507
Email: Unboxedbook@gmail.com
www.unboxedbookproject.com
ISBN: 978-0-9777360-4-1
First Printing, May 2019

TABLE OF CONTENTS

A SPECIAL DEDICATION

This book is dedicated to my mother, the unforgettable,

Ella Chaney Patrick

Her beautiful legacy lives on forever through the thousands of lives touched by the imprint she made on me.

See, Momma, my head is lifted up and I am smiling ...

— *-Dorothy P. Wilson*

FOREWORD

Unboxed is a brilliant read! It is inspiring, soul-stirring, and a powerful reminder that as women our only limitations are those we place on ourselves. We each possess the power to break free from any past or present challenges, hurt, or fears to achieve our ultimate definition of success. The 25 stories in this book will captivate you and reignite your belief that you are indeed a masterpiece with unlimited possibilities to soar.

Cheryl Wood

Cheryl Wood is an international motivational speaker, best-selling author, leadership expert, and America's #1 developer of women speakers. www.cherylempowers.com

INTRODUCTION

When a woman is boxed in, she cannot move because of the people or things in close proximity blocking her way. Being boxed in prevents her from exercising the freedom and capacity she has to soar!

The real problem with being boxed in is that most of the time we don't even realize we are. Have you ever heard the fable about the frog being slowly boiled to death? The premise is that if a frog is put suddenly into boiling water, it would jump out. However, if the frog were put in room temperature water and brought to a slow boil, it wouldn't recognize the danger. Consequently, the frog is cooked to death. As in this metaphor, we can languish in our career, in our life for years, becoming more and more comfortable with being average. Are you in a room-temperature environment yourself, comfortable with being at standard others have set for you?

We can become boxed in by other's definitions of success. We can become boxed in by our past hurts. They keep reminding us that we are nothing special – likely to fail or be hurt again. We can become boxed in by negative words spoken over us, even though the speaker may have been well-meaning.

I remember when I worked in the newspaper industry, I once was told I was a "features person." Meaning, I didn't have the mettle for hard news. Those words chased me for years, forcing me to try to meet someone else's definition of great journalism. I ate that lie and boxed myself in as I tried to be hard like many of the cussing, satirical, bitter journalists around me. What I eventually realized is that what makes me special is not uncovering corruption and toppling politicians; it is discovering and sharing the stories of people who can inspire and empower others to become the best version of themselves.

No longer in the newspaper business, I now publish a women's magazine that connects, celebrates and empowers women.

But that wasn't the only box that held me. As a child, I lived in fear. My father went from a hard-working, fun-loving weekday guy to a binge-drinking, abuse-inflicting weekend monster. The youngest of six children, I watched as my siblings ran away one by one – once they were old enough to find food and a warm bed elsewhere. I remember the awful feeling of sitting there, helplessly unable to help my mother, as her life was threatened by a shotgun to her stomach or revolver to her head. My mother left for good when I was 8 years old, but guess what? Although we fled to the city, that fear still held me hostage, as if I had never left that clapboard house in the country. Fear contained me, keeping me from taking risks, discouraging me from connecting to others, blocking me from the love of others.

Like me, perhaps the biggest box holding you is also fear. Jon Acuff, author of New York Times bestselling book, "Start: Punch Fear in the Face, Escape Average and Do Work that Matters," says, "fear is the most common trap preventing people from reaching their full potential: "I've never met a 20-year-old or a 50-year-old who says, 'I've never had a single passion, dream, hope or desire. We all have them, but a lot of us give in to fear as soon as we get close to them. The reason is that fear only gets loud when you do things that matter. Fear never bothers you if you're average but the second you dare to be more than ordinary, fear awakens."

I finally escaped from the fear box in 1995. I was reading the book of Psalms, Chapter 118, and my thinking was upended forever. "The Lord is with me; I will not be afraid. What can mere mortals do to me?" I ate that truth and it set me free!

My hope is that as you read these powerful words from women who have become unboxed, you will be ready to punch fear in the face, escape average and do work that matters!
My hope is that you'll realize you're a beautiful gift from God, ready to be unboxed to become everything He created you to be. Like a caterpillar metamorphosing into a beautiful butterfly, break free and soar!

Dorothy P. Wilson

Dorothy

Dorothy Patrick Wilson has 30-plus years of experience in publishing, marketing and strategic planning. Originally from Augusta, Ga., she now resides on the Mississippi Gulf Coast with her husband, James.

As a child, Dorothy dreamed of escaping an abusive home life, poverty and fear. Now, her life mission has become to inspire others, particularly women, to break free of past hurts, fear, powerlessness and any other situation that holds them. To this end, she publishes Gulf Coast Woman magazine, and is the co-founder of the Success Women's Conference.

GOD WITHIN ME

By Shelia Rivers

"God is within her!" She will not fall …" — Psalm 46:5

Somewhere deep in your belly you find the strength to press through. There are times you have no idea how you made it from point A to point B.

According to society's theory, I should have been a welfare statistic. I was a single African-American female who had three children by the age of 15 — not to mention, a high school dropout on top of that.

According to statistics, this should have been enough to count me out of beating the odds! The expectation from society was that I would be a welfare recipient and remain as such for the majority of my life. Somehow life has the ability to teach you how to cope with challenging circumstances and come out on the other side. You may have a few scars, but you can come out!

Daily survival and resiliency became my mode of functioning, mentally, physically, and emotionally. Many friends and family would question the madness behind my method of continuous goal setting, then reaching the goals, and challenging myself to achieve the next set of goals. As a young mother, divorced woman, and domestic violence survivor, my experiences were a part of a divinely orchestrated plan. You see, everything I had encountered was a manifestation of greater works to come. Unfortunately, there was no 12-step plan included in this orchestration. It was simply guided by huge leaps of faith. My path toward completing my educational goals over a span of 25 years had been demanding and ever so trying. Yet somehow, I continued to go through the motions, taking one step at a time, one day at a time. I would find myself simply pressing through and living my life by scheduled calendar appointment times. I almost never had a moment to truly enjoy life. My inability to stop and enjoy life resulted in dysfunctional intimate relationships with no level of commitment. I was struggling with my own mental health, including bouts of depression, anxiety, feelings of rejection, and emptiness. During this time my whole life had become nothing more than writing papers, doing homework, research for the homework, occasional church attendance, working dead-end jobs, living from paycheck to paycheck, and caring for my family. This lifestyle had become extremely taxing on my mental health. At this point, a change was necessary. I would've soon needed a straw to breathe because I was surely underwater and drowning fast.

There were days when I would repeat this affirmation numerous times: "God is within her. She will not fall ..." God is within her. She will not fall … . God is within her. She will not fall … ." I knew I had no supernatural control over the doors that were beginning to open in my life, but I swear it felt like one day the sun began to peak through after a lingering hurricane! My hard work was beginning to truly pay off. My education and career licensure afforded me the knowledge and opportunity to start the process of opening my own mental health clinic.

Sometimes life has a way of disrupting our comfort zones. There are times in life when we know that change is necessary for our personal growth. However, we often fail to initiate the change that's required. Somehow the circumstances of life have a way of redirecting our paths.

After the organization I worked for was sold to another company, I was forced to make a decision.

I took a leap of faith and decided to finally use the knowledge and education I had spent numerous years acquiring. After a long hard look at my life, I decided to turn in my resignation and go into business for myself. Needless to say, there was a lot of negative self-talk, ambivalent feelings, and attempts to talk myself out of jumping from a "business owner cliff" with no parachute. To my surprise, it was the best decision I had ever tried to talk myself out of. Over a period of two years, my mental health clinic has skyrocketed! It has grown from single ownership and only being opened late evenings and weekends, to hiring full-time support staff and other clinical team members. Many times, we don't understand the grueling process on the path toward destiny. However, trust that the process is in place to help us reach our goals and prepare us for our divine appointment. For it is in the process that our purpose is discovered, and dreams are realized. Throughout my process, things have not always been crystal clear along the way. There is one thing that I am absolutely sure of; the gift of helping others was divinely ordered by the "God that lives within me! I will not fall … ."

Shelia Rivers

Thank you for always supporting me & being my backbone. I love you.

Failure is not an option

Shelia

Shelia Rivers, a licensed certified social worker, provides counseling services for individuals, children and adolescents, adults, couples, families and groups. She holds a bachelor of science degree in psychology and education, master's in social work and master's in public health-executive administration. She is licensed in Mississippi, Alabama and Louisiana.

Shelia loves making an impact in her family, community and those she has been called to serve.

IT'S TIME TO TURN

By Elaine Stevens

I am a claustrophobic. My irrational fears of being confined make me a poor candidate for space travel. Thank goodness I've never wanted to become an astronaut. There's also the issue of elevators, MRIs, car trunks (remember sneaking into drive-in movies!), or even the third seat of a minivan, especially during rush hour. On occasion, I've been known to get chill bumps and make strange sounds at the mere mention of the word box: n. a rigid typically rectangular container with or without a cover.

Needless to say, being boxed in, crammed, curbed, limited in any capacity, whether it be physically or philosophically, is coffin-like to me. Breaking free from that mindset is being born again.

As a child of the 60s I pride myself on my ideas of freedom. Freedom to be, think, and act as I wish, so long as no one is harmed along the way. In my 70th year I've earned the right to such. However, the journey was difficult.

I lived in many tiny spaces, many boxes, in my mind and in my heart. Some, though minute, were black holes, infinitely imprisoning. I realize I built many of those boxes myself with help, naturally, from the wonderful four-letter word: LIFE. Family and colleagues assisted in the construction. I guess you could say over time I've lived in a subdivision of boxes. Fear, insecurity, sadness, and conformity to name a few. Some were created for safety. "If I can hide in this box, maybe no one will see me for who I really am." Or, "My box allows me sanctuary from the storms of failure. I'll just stay where I am."

Poet Mary Oliver said, "Someone I loved once gave me a box full of darkness. It took me years to understand that this too was a gift." I clearly remember mine. It happened in my youth. A tragic accident, the death of the father of my daughter who was adopted by someone far away. The box of darkness became my path to self-discovery and to experiencing more love in my life than I could ever have imagined, including the love of my daughter who I found thirty-five years later.

This is my favorite: "You can't go to New York and become a dancer or do anything there for that matter. We won't allow it." Boxed in by culture, a primeval culprit. I went to New York in the 70s. I didn't become a dancer. Instead, I found my truest calling. I literally stepped into a HUGE box, watched by millions worldwide: television! I started my industry career with Dick Cavett in New York. From there I came home to Biloxi and became the female anchor of the first all-female news team in the nation along with the esteemed Robin Roberts.

Choreographer and dancer, Twyla Tharp, said, "Before you can think out of the box, you have to start with a box." I suppose, in a way, some of our boxes are our GPS to our ultimate potential, the purpose we seek. Boxes have a Siri, too! You just have to listen to the voice within which says, "It's time to turn here now!"

Elaine Stevens

Elaine

Elaine Stevens is an award-winning public relations and media veteran. Her career includes radio and television broadcasting, investigative news reporting and anchoring, documentary and television news series production, development of original programming, and on-air hosting of her own local television program Art Beat: The Heartbeat of South Mississippi. Elaine's broadcasting profession has taken her cross country from New York City the Dick Cavett Show in the late 1970s on public television to San Diego, Calif., in 1995 where she owned and operated Stevens Media Productions & Consulting.

Her creative essay, "Cookies for Breakfast," won first place with the 2018 Mary Helen Washington Writing Contest of Marygrove College, Detroit, Mich., and was short listed for the 2017 William Faulkner Words & Music Literary Festival, New Orleans.

Elaine has co-authored two biographies "Chameleon: hanging by my tale" by Edward Fassel and "The True Art of Living in America by Art Sapanli". She is currently working on her memoir "Mermaid in the Window" and a compilation of short stories titled, "I Married the Waterman: Southern Tales of Love & Woe". Elaine has written for several publications.

LIFE IS FULL OF POSSIBILITIES

By Dorothy Roberts

My parents, the late Lawrence and Lucimarian Roberts of Pass Christian, Miss. instilled in my siblings and I, the values of integrity, faith in God, resilience, and service. Along with my brother, Butch, and sisters, Sally-Ann and Robin, we admired our parents as we watched them emulate those qualities before us. My parents went through each season of their entire lives, teaching and sharing these values with us and others.

The first part of my career spanned a total of 28 years. I started out as a music teacher and then became a social worker for individuals with developmental disabilities. The work was challenging but very rewarding. You see, my mother wanted me to be a music teacher. So, I matriculated from William Carey University with an undergraduate degree in Music Education. However, as I taught children music, I always felt I needed to do more. "Doing more" was a constant factor in my life. As the daughter of an Air Force officer and Howard University graduate, expectations to achieve were sometimes subtle but always present in conversations with my parents.

I decided on the field of social work, (which was my mother's first work) after meeting a medical social worker in a hospital where I was employed. As I looked into this course of study, I realized that my life experience that was leading me to this choice. I decided to pursue a master's degree in social work. I actually felt called into this profession. A profession that revolved around helping people through life's challenges. Although it is much more than simply helping people. It's about meeting people on their level and assisting with the services they need to move forward in life. It's about advocating for those whose voices aren't recognized and giving people hope when they have none.

During my years as a social worker in a state-operated program, I often involved myself with artistic endeavors. Maybe expressing myself through art, was my way of coping with the stress of my profession. I have always enjoyed making gifts for family and friends. It's just an innate part of me to create. I simply love the art of making things! On a trip one Sunday afternoon to Bay St. Louis with girlfriends who were supporting me through a divorce after 25 years of marriage, I came across a bead shop. I don't know which captured me first, the colors of the beads as they shone on the glass shelves in the shop, the classes offered to help you learn the art of jewelry making or the endless possibilities of what could be made. This is where I fell in love with jewelry making.

"Just For You Jewelry" was the first business I established as I polished my techniques of jewelry making. It was therapy as I grieved the ending of my marriage. As I designed pieces, I would think of the person who would enjoy wearing my creations. It gave me such a sense of accomplishment as I would design a new necklace or pair of earrings. My sisters, Sally-Ann and Robin wore many of my pieces on their respective morning TV shows; CBS in New Orleans and Good Morning America in New York. I have to admit, I always enjoyed seeing them wearing one of my necklaces or a pair of earrings. I received such support from sales at festivals and an online store, that I soon displayed my work in a local gallery.

In 2012 our family was hit with a double whammy! Our mother had a massive stroke in July and passed on Aug. 30, 2012. In addition, our beloved baby sister, Robin, had developed a serious side-effect of chemotherapy called MDS, from her previous treatment for breast cancer. If Robin wasn't able to receive a bone marrow transplant, we would also lose our sister. It was a dark time for our family. We faced these two major challenges with the resilience our parents had taught us. We relied on our faith and embraced the prayers of a community who loved our baby sister. It was a blessing that Sally-Ann was a perfect match for Robin!

When faced with these challenges, I began to look at the brevity of life. While I had enjoyed my work as a social worker administrator, I began to think about what I would do in retirement during the fall season of my life. I had always thought it was good to retire to something. My parents demonstrated that to me and my siblings through the seasons of their lives. Dad had an illustrious military career while my mom looked after the household. She moved our family over 20 times in his 30-year career! When dad retired, mom's career of community building began. She was appointed to numerous local, state and national boards. It was dad's time to travel with mom as she met her board responsibilities. So quite naturally, it was in me to retire to another career.

In September 2015, just six weeks after retiring from state service, I opened Robin's Nest in the Pass, a gallery gift shop in Pass Christian, Miss. At Robin's Nest, you'll find artisan jewelry, local art, pottery, glassware, accessories, bath and body collections and gifts for all occasions. Our mission is to "celebrate the creative spirit!" It's not just a gift shop, but a shop where we support local artists who have a venue to display and sell their art.

Going from social work to becoming a retail business owner came with some challenges and anxiety (as one could imagine). It's one thing to sell your work at a festival and quite another to stock a 1,000 square foot retail store.

Along the journey, people crossed my path who were willing to share their expertise in marketing, retail, and finances.

The one common recommendation made was to hire someone else. Running a store by yourself was too difficult apparently. You have to surround yourself with people who have skill sets you don't have. You can feel quite vulnerable when you realize you don't know what you don't know!

Having a foundation of faith brought me through moments of uncertainty. I attended classes offered by the Small Business Administration to fill in the gaps. The information I learned helped me to establish the necessary financial and legal aspects related to running a business. I was learning a new set of lingo ... LLC, EIN, Resale ID, etc. The local SBA folks are a wonderful resource for people interested in opening a business.

Along this journey, God has always placed the right people, at the right time in my path. Of course, having sisters in the national and regional spotlight has brought to me a base of people who want to visit the store. Having a built-in audience is wonderful and I am truly blessed to have this. But it's also a bit daunting too. That little inner voice of insecurity can creep in to say, I wonder if people will like what we offer at Robin's Nest or will they be disappointed. I quell that inner voice by allowing the larger and deeper voice of God to resonate within me. I believe when you are in the flow of your passion, God will allow the gift he has bestowed upon you, to spill forth!

This has been a tremendously enjoyable season of life for me, as I was fortunate to remarry in 2016! I absolutely love all aspects of being in retail. Yes, it can be exhausting at times, but when a customer comes in and says they love the atmosphere in the store, the wonderful selection of merchandise and they feel uplifted after being there, it gives me energy!

Opening Robin's Nest in the Pass was the first of two other projects I plan to establish. I believe Lawrence and Lucimarian Roberts would be pleased to see their family is a part of the business community, in a town they dearly loved. I can truly say, life is full of possibilities!

Dorothy Roberts

Dorothy

Dorothy Roberts retired from the State of Mississippi in, 2015, after 28 years of service. As a licensed certified social worker, Dorothy's career revolved around working with individuals with developmental disabilities and their families. On September 18, 2015, she opened a gallery gift shop called Robin's Nest in the Pass. The gallery gift shop was established in the small town of Pass Christian, Miss., to honor her sister, Robin Roberts, and her parent's love for this quaint coastal town. Dorothy has created jewelry worn by her sisters, Sally-Ann Roberts, former anchor of WWL-TV4 Morning Show in New Orleans and Robin Roberts, anchor of ABC Good Morning America.

Dorothy is the mother of two daughters, Jessica McEwen and Lauren Hinton, the grandmother of two grandsons, Ryan and Lawrence Hinton and granddaughter, Dovie Strickland. She is married to Mr. Halle Ricketts of Grenada, Miss. They reside in Pass Christian, Miss.

A HEART TO SERVE
By Sherry Owen

Who knew that a single mom with children would be the catalyst that God would use to cause me to branch out into my own business? I had worked real estate for almost 18 years with one of the most successful agencies in our community. I always loved the work I did, but I knew there was more to real estate than just selling homes, at least for me.

So when the young mom came to me to buy a home, everything was set in place. She wanted something more for her family and to set an example for her children. As a mom, I could totally relate to her. What we didn't expect were the additional fees that she would have to cover to move from apartment living to a homeowner. I don't know what was so different about this client - maybe it was because she was a single mom trying to better herself, or just maybe it was that push I needed to stand for what I believed in.

I remember the situation so vividly. I went to the ballpark where my husband was out on the field playing ball. I walked right out onto the field waving that contract in my hand and asked him to look at it for me. I must have been a sight, but I was on a mission. I wanted to know my options and how I could help this single mom from a legal standpoint. Well, God worked it out and we got her moved in, but in the process, He birthed a vision in me that would lead to the business I've been fortunate enough to operate without sacrificing my relationship with God and my family.

I admit I had my reservations, as anyone would leaving a successful business with an agency to branch out and build their own, but I was committed. I watched, I learned, and I put in the work, and within two years I had amassed success that I didn't know was available to me.

All I knew is that I wanted to help people because I cared about them and not because they were a dollar sign in my eyes. As I began to serve from a place of love, my business grew. I had agents reach out to me who wanted to join my company. Eventually, architects would contact me to develop partnerships. I trusted God with my business, and it continued to grow by leaps and bounds.

Like any business, I've experienced my share of challenges, but it has been worth it to know that I'm able to not only help single moms, but other individuals become first-time homeowners without the stress associated with buying a home.

It's not always about numbers and volume, but about having a passion for what it is that you do. It's about having a life and being able to set parameters about what you allow. You create your own freedom, like choosing to not work on the weekend.

I look back and I'm grateful that I took a stand to make a difference in the lives of others and my own life. I made the decision early on that my life would consist of God, family and then real estate.

I became unboxed when I made the decision to serve from a place of love … . That's the key to unlocking your dreams.

Sherry Owen

Sherry

Sherry is a leader in both residential and commercial real estate along the Mississippi Gulf Coast. Her keen business sense, incredible eye for design, and innovative marketing strategies have helped to identify her as a leader in high-end residential home sales.

Sherry is known for her commitment to her clients, professionalism, and knowledge of the Mississippi Gulf Coast.

A long-time resident with deep family roots, the Mississippi Gulf Coast is her home and she loves introducing newcomers to all the Coast has to offer.

LIVING TO THRIVE

By Tiffany D. Bell

I remember my first-time visiting Flint Creek. It was a very bright and sunny day. It was about a 25-minute drive from my house. Having never been there, my boys, who were ages 4 and 12 at the time, were pretty excited. None of us were sure what to expect. My idea of a creek was a stream of brown water that filled a ditch alongside a dirt road with tadpoles. Surely that was nothing to get overly excited about. It was the day of our church's annual picnic. We had been attending the church for about a year and a half and had made a few friends. We made plans to attend the picnic together that day at the creek. So, my boys and I packed a picnic basket, grabbed a few blankets, towels, drinks, sunscreen and hit the road.

Turns out, Flint Creek was not a ditch of dirty water and tadpoles at all! It's a 650-acre lake with 13 miles of shoreline stocked with all kinds of fish. Thousands of people flood there over the year to enjoy camping, boating, picnicking and more. And it was finally our turn. The kids waited patiently for our car to get to the front of the line to pay for entry. I can still picture the excitement in Brandon's eyes. He always had lots of questions. Brieyon, on the other hand, had very little questions. He would rather begin exploring and ask questions later. We pulled up to check in, paid our entry fee, and followed to possession of other car riders as they made their way into the park.

As we waited for the traffic to begin to move again, I looked up to see a hill covered in beautiful plush green grass. The sky was clear. It was a beautiful shade of blue. I had not taken notice of the sky or anything dealing with nature in while. There was gentle breeze blowing and the temperature was perfect. As I looked around and took in the beauty of our surroundings, I felt the warmth of hope and assurance arise for the first time in weeks. That one hill lead into another hill, some filled with trees, others covered in plush green grass. Other hills were covered with smiling faces of families and friends enjoying each other. I am really not sure how to describe that moment, but I felt alive for the first time in weeks. I felt as if I were looking up for the very first time and that I could see something other than responsibility, fear, or questions. Again, I don't have words to describe how I felt.

What you are not aware of is that my husband died several weeks prior. It was sudden and unexpected. He was injured on the job. I do remember that day in vivid detail. I remember waking up that morning, with him sitting beside me on the bed. I can still feel his hand rubbing my back tenderly telling me that it was time to get up and get the day started. The room was dimly lit. He seemed worried. I could feel his stress about what day would bring. I assured him that things would fall into to place and that it would all work out. He was worried about being able to complete the job on time because he had lost an employee the day before.

I got up and dressed for the day as normal. He took out youngest son to school and I took our oldest. Before hopping in the car to leave, I struggled mentally on whether or not to stop and give him a kiss or to hurry and get in the car to head out. I did not want to be late for work. I honestly don't remember what I choose to do. What I do remember was that I struggled all day to stay at work. I wanted to speak to him. I called several times but there was never an answer. I had no idea that when I said goodbye to him that morning that it would be my last time saying goodbye. Eventually, I asked my boss to leave work early. I knew in my heart that I had to find Ken. Where was he working that day? I had no idea. All I knew is that I had to find him.

I grabbed my purse and keys, clocked out and headed for my car. I drove over one block and called him. I had called him several times that day, he was not able to answer. After the third unanswered call, I left him a message saying that I loved him. Finally, there was an answer. But, it wasn't his voice. It was an emergency room nurse. The next voice that I heard was an ER physician telling me that my husband had just died. The doctor had done all that he could to save him but was unsuccessful. He told me to grab my boys and come to say goodbye. I cannot describe the state of shock, fear, disappointment, and uncertainty that I felt at that moment. The only thing that I knew was that I needed to make sure that my boys were going to be okay. They became my driving force and passion. In my heart, my goal was to survive. Grief and responsibility became my box.

Surviving a good thing, but there is more to life than surviving. I believe that God wants us to do more than survive tragedy or heartache. I believe that He wants us the thrive. I believe that there is life after death, literally and figuratively. How was I going to live from day to day without my husband and father to my children? How were we going to survive financially? Boys need a male role model in their lives, especially when the entered teenage years. How would survive emotionally? All of these questions consumed me during the first few weeks after his accident.

The day at Flint Creek opened my eyes. I was not aware that I had allowed myself to become boxed in. I really didn't realize that I was not planning to thrive, but only to survive. Seeing the beauty of nature and seeing other people smiling enjoying life and each other really helped to open my eyes. Sometimes life sends things at you that are not fair. There are unexpected twists and turns, potholes even, that don't line up with the way we envision life going. Deciding to survive is a great first step. But deciding to thrive afterward is even better. I decided that I would live again. That I would see my kids smile again at the memory of their dad. Yes, there will be tender moments, which should be treasured too.

Even as I write this, 12e years later, I have had to wipe a few tears away, but I am grateful for these memories. But there will also be moments that we should cherish and celebrate. I decided to be intentional to create memories with my children that would overshadow moments of pain and disappointments. My boys have many, many stories to share about our silly days as a family. The hills at Flint Creek became an inspiration for me. I was determined to create a life for me and my children that filled with green grass, a few trees for shade and rest, and people that we would treat as family. We would laugh and cry at times, but no longer live in the shadow of grief or focus on what was. Instead, in order to thrive, I began to look for a way to rewrite our future with love, laughter, and people that share it with. I looked for opportunities to hope again.

I refused to live under the label of a single parent or even a widow. Everyone would know Tiffany to be a mother, a friend, and a servant to others.

Take whatever life sends your way as an opportunity to create a new beginning, a new future, and new you!

Tiffany D. Bell

Tiffany

Tiffany D. Bell is the executive director of the Women's Resource Center. Tiffany serves on the Board of Directors of the Biloxi Bay Area Chamber and Lighthouse Business Professional Women. She also serves as co-director of the Success Women's Conference and as a member of the Orange Grove Kiwanis Club.

FROM POSITION TO PURPOSE

By Robin Killeen

The year was 1988 when I started my position in the staffing industry as a sales consultant. Within two years, I was promoted to branch manager and by 1992 I was promoted to the position of Regional Manager. I knew the industry like the back of my hand and could run it with my eyes closed. I worked 60 to 80 hours a week and experienced much success. The time and dedication I put in, helped me achieved an impressive title, with a large team and a great compensation package. I was outwardly successful, but inwardly unfulfilled.

With all my professional success, how could I possibly be discontent? Unfulfilled? What components were missing from my life? In 1994 I found exactly what was missing and I re-dedicated my life to God. My mindset began to shift, I wanted to be the best me that He had in mind when He created me.

So with that shift, I was still in the regional manager position but now desiring to walk in my God designed purpose. That was when I begin to realize I was boxed in. How could I consider giving up a position that took me years to achieve success in, only to move into unfamiliar territory. I was safe, comfortable and financially sound.

Fast-forward to May 2012. That was the day I became unboxed - my position was eliminated. On that day, I unplugged and drove away leaving everything I had worked so hard to build in my rearview mirror. I left my title, my employees that I considered friends and my hefty compensation. I knew it would be a big adjustment financially, never mind the thought of what I would do to fill those hours I spent at work. During this period, I had many regrets. The long hours I had put in and all those things outside of work that I missed. The story that I had heard so many times, that when you are on your deathbed no one ever says, I wished I would have spent more time at the office, rang loud in my mind.

Time is our one common currency. We have each been given 24 hours in the day, and it's up to us to choose how to spend them. While transitioning from position to purpose, I utilized this to trigger an internal investigation on who I was outside of my former position. What were my passions and desires that would bring me the greatest fulfillment? I asked myself questions such as; had my position become my identity? I was now in a state of becoming unboxed, unmasked, and untangled.

In life we are bombarded by doubts and fears that many times keep us from living out the purposes God established for us. Letting go and walking in your purpose requires courage. Courage is not the absence of fear; it is doing what you are called to do in spite of fear.

Fast-forward to today. God has blessed me with valuable time to spend with family, friends as well as time to grow W.O.W (Women of Wisdom). by empowering and encouraging women in our community and beyond. I've been blessed to now buy neglected houses transform them into a beautiful dream home ready for a new family to enjoy.

I now understand that the road toward God's purpose for my life will not always be lined with roses. Looking back now, I'm able to see the blessings in those times of the painful pruning. Now with my passion shifted, my main goal is to fulfill His purpose for my life.

I am truly unboxed! I am living and working in collaboration with God, walking in His purpose and sometimes that feels very unnatural and uncomfortable. He is the architect; I am only the builder. 2 Corinthians 12:9 says, "But he said to me, 'My grace is sufficient for you, for my power is made perfect in weakness.' "

Mark Zuckerberg says, "purpose is that sense that we are a part of something bigger than ourselves." Purpose is what creates true happiness and contentment.

2 Timothy 1:9 says, "We are called according to His purpose." There is great joy in discovering His purpose for our lives. Especially when we trust in Him rather than in our own feelings or expectations from others. To know our purpose is to know who we are and what we are created to do. Do you know your purpose?

Well that's my story from my position to His purpose! God is writing your story too. He has a plan and a purpose just for you! Walk in it and experience freedom!

Robin Killeen

Robin

Robin Killeen is founder of W.O.W. (Women of Wisdom) it was established on the Gulf Coast in 1999 as "Christian marketplace ministry" with a 3C mission: connect, create, cultivate. March of Dimes, American Cancer Society and the Society for Human Resource Management are a handful of organizations she has been involved in.

She also has been a part of the Biloxi Bay Chamber of Commerce and has served in various positions from ambassador to president. She left the staffing industry to pursue an adventure with her daughter where they flip houses by transforming neglected homes to make it a gem again for a new family.

UNBOX YOUR PURPOSE

By Kearn Cherry

Sometimes in life, we feel boxed in. We don't recognize or know how to use our God-given gifts. Oftentimes, we view our goals as too hard to accomplish so we put it in a "box" in our mind and never finish it. We all have been blessed with gifts, but sometimes we box them up, store them away and forget about them. My gifts are connecting with people and empowering others. As a young mother at 19 years old, I had previously aspired to join my brother in the field of engineering, but that was not to be. I made the decision to pursue nursing because I felt that was the more practical choice now that I was a mother. It appeared to be the appropriate career path for me.

I began working at a medical clinic while attending college for nursing when my son was just three weeks old. Shortly after my son's father and I got married, he headed off to Germany in the military. As a young wife, I felt my duty was to join my husband. So, I decided to put my dreams of entering the nursing program on hold. Never thinking five years would pass before I could finish my nursing degree. After returning to the states, I decided to "dust off the box" and continue my path toward a nursing degree. Yes, this is always a mental battle because you start thinking "Is this really what I want to do?" Well, of course, it is! At least that's what I thought.

When we landed in Sierra Vista, Ariz., I had no idea the town had a population of only 15,000, but I was determined this was the place to finish my goal of becoming a nurse. After settling in, I headed to the only college in town to apply for their nursing program. Thinking that since I already had my associate degree in liberal arts with an emphasis in nursing, this should be a breeze. However, the school had more than 600 people on the waiting list. Even worse, it only accepted 65 students each year. What a nightmare! I asked myself, "Is this what I really wanted to do?"

So once again, I mentally put everything in a box. I had to work. I had three kids to feed and my husband was getting out of the military. My thoughts were all over the place. I knew that I was meant to be in the medical field. So, I began working multiple jobs, one being a nursing aide. I had to earn a living, but I knew there had to be something more in store for me. Still very young, my husband and I decided to travel to Tucson, Ariz., which was an hour and a half drive one way to apply for their nursing program. Surely there had to be more opportunities in Tucson. However, we were surprised to find there were no openings in their nursing programs either. This served as a sign that we were being led in a different direction. We then heard about an occupational therapy program, and that is the path we took. This eventually led to us opening PRN Home Care, which has been in operation for 22 years. We provide resources to individuals, enabling them to remain at home and enjoy a better quality of life.

God has a funny way of showing us that our purpose may not be what we envision. Though I am not currently working in occupational therapy, it did assist me in finding my purpose of empowering and encouraging caregivers and women. Sometimes the path to our purpose may not be straightforward or clear.

There may be detours, roadblocks, or a long hiatus. I also learned that God guides our steps, and everyone has a purpose or calling. You must recognize and acknowledge your GOD-GIVEN PURPOSE.

Don't leave your gifts in a box on a shelf. UNBOX YOUR GIFTS AND START WALKING IN YOUR PURPOSE!

Kearn Cherry

Kearn

Kearn Cherry is vice president of operations/co-owner of PRN Home Care. Kearn started her career in therapy. After living abroad in Germany and moving to Sierra Vista, Ariz., she started her first business and completed her second degree in occupational therapy. After working a few years as an occupational therapist, the vision for PRN Staffing and PRN Home Care were created.

As a business owner, Kearn believes that you must be a community leader. She has served as a board member for the Chamber of Commerce, and on other committees such as American Heart Association, Lighthouse Business & Professional Women, Mental Health Association, Gulf Coast Symphony Orchestra. She co-founded the Success Women's Conference and was instrumental in the creation of Blessed Gyrls Rock Conference. She founded the R.I.P.E. Conference and Senior Prom.

Kearn currently brings her talents to television with her show, "Unwrinkled Heart Caregivers' Journeys," to homes on the Mississippi Gulf Coast.

BREAKING FREE

By Holly Lemoine-Raymond

Have you ever been stuck in a rut? You know that place. The one where you are on autopilot and everything is mundane. This was the case when I worked the same casino job for over 18 years. I loved what I did. I loved my clients. The job was challenging and fun. But after a while, you just feel "stuck." That's where I was … Stuck. I felt comfortable. I could do that job in my sleep. I always drove the same route, day after day, just going from "A" to "B" and "B" to "A". I never went another route. I was "boxed in" and I needed to break free. I needed to do something different. Anything.

When I finally left the casino, I felt lost. I was no longer driving that same old route. I was confused and out of place. I didn't know which way to go. For the first time in over 18 years, I did not have to work every weekend, holiday, early morning or late night. But what should I do? What could I do? I felt like I had gone through a bad break up of a long, meaningful relationship.

I had a lot of ideas floating around in my mind. There were things I wanted to do, but I didn't know where to start. I needed to re-invent myself. I felt like I hit rock bottom in my professional life. I needed to remove the self-imposed limitations that kept me in the safety net of the casino world.

"Not till we are lost do we begin to find ourselves again."
— Henry David Thoreau

I thought about the advice my mother had given me so many years ago. She always encouraged me to pursue my bucket list. She always told me not to let anyone discourage me. Remembering those words of wisdom, I told myself that I couldn't just sit around and be depressed!

In between my careers, I took time out to reflect on my life and figure out who I was and what I wanted. I took the opportunity to do some things I wanted to do, like swimming with Great White Sharks in the Farallon Islands, just off the coast of San Francisco. I traveled to Europe and fell in love with Italy! I opened my own café there. I called it "Cypress Café." I also started to rescue animals on my 43-acre farm in Picayune, MS. Every time I checked something off my bucket list, I gained more confidence. I started to find myself and my healing had begun.

In my time of self-discovery, I heard my mom saying, "Always do your best and be the best person you can be. When you do something for yourself, make sure you also do for others." I was inspired, once again, by my mother's voice. I worked with the city of Bay St. Louis on the 5 Years Forward, a tribute commemorating how far we had come after Hurricane Katrina. I contributed to the restoration of the Duck Pond in Bay St. Louis. I volunteered with the Animal Shelter and mentored local youth. Every time I did something I wanted to do, I found ways to give back to the community. I started to feel energized. I found a new way to serve others. This is when I realized I was becoming "unboxed!"

I felt like a new person. This was my chance to really be who I was. I've always had a passion for television, real estate, and interior design. After opening and operating a successful café in Bay St. Louis, I yearned for more.

My mom retired from being the principal of a school in New Orleans and became a real estate agent in Destin, Fla. After she passed away, I decided to follow in her footsteps and get into Real Estate. I joined a local, highly respected brokerage. With a lot of hard work and dedication, I became a top producing agent. Yet I still wanted more. I went back to school to get my real estate broker's license. I then took a leap of faith and opened HL Raymond Properties, a "boutique" real estate brokerage. From working for a local broker to starting my own brokerage, the ride has been non-stop.

A couple of years ago, I got a call from HGTV to do an episode of "Beachfront Bargain Hunt" and started filming months later. The producers of "You Live in What?", on the Great American Country Network, filmed the gas station I had converted into an industrial-chic get-a-way. About a year later, I filmed an episode with them. Most recently, I was contacted by other production companies to do my own series, but nothing fit. It took my attention away from my clients and I needed to refocus on my business. The success from "Beach Front Bargain Hunt" and "You Live in What?" fueled the fire for me to produce my own television show.

With many years in the making, I finally have my own television series called "Inside Out with HL Raymond Properties." It's a new, unique approach to a Home TV Series. This worked for me because I was able to do it in my own time and incorporate HL Raymond Properties. I acquired some unique DIY projects and new clients. The series airs each Sunday on several different channels throughout the region. It's a self-produced program showcasing our beautiful Mississippi Gulf Coast properties and all the Coast has to offer. With new plans to film season two, my bucket list is beginning to fill up again.

With the trials and tribulations, I have faced, I've learned that sometimes you have to step back, take a deep breath, and begin again. While finding myself, I remembered to help others as my mother had always told me. Everything I have ever done in my professional and personal life has brought me to where I am today, and I'm not done yet.

Holly Lemoine-Raymond

Holly

Holly Lemoine-Raymond is executive producer of the TV series "Inside Outside with HL Raymond Properties" and the broker, owner and designer of HL Raymond Properties, LLC in Bay Saint Louis, Miss.

After being in real estate for less than two years, Holly got her broker's license and ventured out on her own and created HL Raymond Properties, LLC. She was featured many times on HGTV, which lead to the production of her own real estate TV series. Holly likes to spend time with her husband Leo and son, Landry.

LABELS

By Keva Scott

I was in the sixth grade and my English teacher was giving out copies of the poem, "If" by Rudyard Kipling. She was looking to select a student to read this poem in the school assembly. She had passed out copies of the poem to the class but somehow skipped me. I went to her after class and asked if I could have a copy because I wanted to read the poem, too. She looked at me and said, "You? Your bad self? Oh, no. Besides this is for students who will read in the assembly and you know you can't do that." Little did she know that my grandmother, a librarian and voracious reader, had taught me this poem (and many others) when I was 8 years old and I recited it frequently at home.

I was labeled a "bad child." Now I admit raising me was no easy task! I had a strong will, I always saw and chose a different path, and I was very direct and honest. When pushed, I pushed back, with no fear. Academically, I could compete with my peers but those behaviors, as it were, landed me with the label, "Bad Child". This label stayed with me for years. This label walked in the room before I ever entered. This label met people before I ever had the chance to. This label caused adults to prepare for me rather than get to know me. Finally, I was diagnosed with ADHD (Attention Deficit Hyperactive Disorder) and since this was a fairly new label, they didn't know what to do with me, so in the sixth grade, I was placed in a special education class. I may have been strong-willed, but I didn't have a learning disability. It was recommended that I would be mainstreamed or allowed to go back to regular classes with my peers when I learned to act "just like them." In other words, when my strong will was broken.

In this class, I was doing my work and helping the teachers with the other students. Because I believed I was bad, I didn't think good things were meant for me.

Labels are "limiting boxes" that we dump people inside of when we fail to understand them. Over 400 years ago, alchemist and physician, Paracelsus said, "All substances are poisons; there is none that is not a poison." Meaning everything good has a little bad if it is too much. It's the dosage that determines if it is, in fact, poison or a remedy.

A substance that's considered poison in one state of being can become a remedy in another state. For instance, many don't know that the apple contains cyanide. Cyanide is a rapidly acting deadly poison. However, in a small dosage, as in the case of an apple, it maintains healthy nerve and red blood cells (an apple a day keeps the doctor away). If we label the apple as bad, based solely on the small trace of cyanide we miss out on the wonderful health benefits the apple gives us. The right amount in the right context becomes a remedy.

My mother named me Keva, meaning "protected" and JaHan, meaning, "gift of God." No matter what the world called me when I got home my family called me who I was destined to be, a "protected gift." The world defined me based on the small dosage of bad that was inside of me, but in the right context, I became a remedy for the world. Those who know me well, know that I'm still that same little girl. I still have that strong will. Although now my strong will has been relabeled "tenacity." Being determined, focused, and unwilling to quit allowed me the ability to lead through difficulty and change. My strong will, (or "tenacity" as it has been relabeled) allowed me to ... fail and start again.

I still see and choose a different path! This has been relabeled "innovative." It is my innovation that has given me the ability to come into an organization and transform it by seeing opportunities where others saw problems. I am still direct and honest. Now, relabeled open. My honest communication has allowed me to establish effective work teams that are built on trust, with the ability to accomplish tasks with no hidden agendas. The substances that once negatively labeled me have now relabeled me a "leader." Over the last 22 years, I have been blessed to lead many teams, and oversee hundreds of staff members in six different states in my youth development career. I've created programs and projects that will outlive me. These programs have impacted countless youth across the nation. These innate traits once labeled as "bad" have become the keys to unlock my success.

Though the world tried to put me in its box and label me as poison…I became a remedy. We must break free of the labels placed on us by people and allow God to relabel us for destiny!

Keva Scott

Keva

As the chief executive officer of the Boys & Girls Clubs of the Gulf Coast, Keva is a dynamic leader that hit the ground running when she took over as CEO of a struggling organization in 2015. Keva earned a B.A. in Communications and Business from Auburn University, a master's in business organizational development from Regent University in Virginia Beach, Va., and an education specialist (Ed.S.) from Auburn University.

Keva has designed many programs to reach at-risk youth, received millions of dollars in program grants and has partnered with over 150 different organizations/businesses. She has trained more than 1,200 staff and volunteers, which enabled her to touch the lives of more than 10,000 young people with programs and services in her 22-year career in youth development. Keva is committed to seeing that all young people reach their full potential through mentoring, workforce development, and eliminating poverty.

LIVING THE DREAM
By Jessica Williams

When I was a young girl, I dreamed of one day wearing a business suit and heels, walking around my oversized office with a view of the coastline. I wanted to be the boss lady, to own the company and rule the world from my desk on the top floor. My focus became studying business and landing a role in the corporate world.

Yet there I was, 27 years old and five years into my ideal corporate position when I decided to surrender it all to become a stay at home momma and homeschool my children.

It wasn't until after having our second son that I found myself wanting a different dream and a different vision. I would spend my days dreaming about something different. Rather than focusing on projects and deadlines, I was having visions of days where I was no longer rushing out of the door before 7 a.m., but rather staying home soaking up every moment with my children. My desires changed from climbing the corporate ladder to taking care of my family. Mother Theresa said, "If you want to change the world, go home and love your family." That's exactly what I wanted to do.

I know that God gave me this unique calling to serve my family in this way. It was never a part of my plan; however, I found myself wanting nothing more. So, after a few months of having this dream tug at my heartstrings, I made the transition from corporate life to the home life.

As you can imagine, everyone had an opinion about my decision." Why leave a financially secure job?" "You're going to depend solely on your husband's income?" "What if something happens and you're left with no job?" "Homeschooling your children will make them weird and unsocialized." "You don't have a teaching degree."

Most of these opinions came from women. Women, who were typically supportive, empowering, and encouraging to other women. So why was my situation any different? Was I supposed to stay at a job because society says that's the new norm for women nowadays? Was I supposed to allow others opinions and views to determine my own?

You know, I don't think I would have had such resistance if I was changing roles to obtain monetary success or a notable title on the corporate ladder. Those are applauded changes and congratulatory movements in most people's opinions. I was making the unpopular choice, to give it all up to change the world ... starting in my very own home.

My dreams may look different than yours and that's because they're mine. Your dreams will look different than anyone else's because they are yours!

Along the way, I have learned not to let anyone's opinion of my dreams make me feel inferior. My dream carried many risks, but I knew the risk was worth taking.

Years after making the decision to leave my corporate job, I finally understood the purpose behind my calling. Our oldest son became extremely ill and was diagnosed with Ulcerative

Colitis, an inflammatory bowel, and autoimmune disease. For three years he was fighting this terrible disease with wavering health and he needed my care more than ever before. Thankfully, his disease has since been cured through surgery and the purpose of my calling has never been more transparent.

Today, my husband and I own A.J. Williams Media, LLC., a fast-growing media company in South Mississippi. I currently specialize in video production. From time to time, I do wear a business suit and heels, but most days I can be found in yoga pants at home, balancing my priorities of family and work. My dreams are no longer to run the corporate but to be a healthy woman that responds to God's calling on her life. I'm going to be who I'm called to be with no hesitation and no fear. I am completely willing to take the risk.

Jessica Williams

Jessica

Jessica Williams has been married to Anthony Williams for 10 years and they have three children Jayden 15, Jude, 8, and Joslyn, 4. Jessica and her husband own A.J. Williams Media, LLC, a fast-growing media company specializing in videography.

In addition to running their company, Jessica also home-schools their three children. She believes in enjoying life and letting her hair do it's thing, wearing yoga pants even when she's not working out, and spoiling her diet on sushi or guacamole.

Jessica is passionate about Jesus and encourages women to push past the walls around them.

THE REAL LATISHA

By Latisha Lewis Price

One summer afternoon while working at the Sun Herald newspaper, I received a phone call from a woman with a Southern accent. I answered, "Thank you for calling the Sun Herald Advertising Department, how may I help you?" She said, "Who are you?" I said, "I'm Latisha Price; she said once again, "Who are you?" I said, "I'm Latisha Price and I work for the Advertising director." She said again very slowly in her Julia Sugarbaker's voice, "Who... are... you?" At that moment I realized I did not know who I was or my purpose in life. The rest of that day seemed blank for me because I was wondering to myself, "Who are you Latisha?" For months, I was asking myself that question. I did not know how to find Latisha. You see, I lost myself helping my family, friends, and building the dreams of others. That's how I identified myself.

Who are you? Who Are You? WHO ARE YOU? I wrote those words on my mirror and I just stared at those words wondering who is Latisha? I begin reading books on faith, personal development, and the law of attraction looking for Latisha. I was looking for me as if I was physically lost. It was much worse; I was mentally lost; I allowed others to shape me.

I am the middle child and was a people pleaser. I did everything to please my mother and wanted her to be so proud of me. This part of my life is where I began to get boxed in. I held everything in, emotions, feelings, ideas, thoughts, and most of all, myself. I did not have a voice and I felt invisible at times. When I spoke, no one heard me. I allowed the voice of others to be the loudest for me. While I was helping others build their dreams, I allowed them to fight for me. I did not know how to fight for myself. At that time in my life I had absolutely no grit. I thought I hid it well; I just wanted people to like me. I thought I put on a good front but on the inside, there was no substance. Going through this I lost courage, confidence, and faith. I quit everything I started, I would procrastinate on projects, and I did not keep my word. Looking back on that period in my life, I realized I was tired and ready to break out of the box I allowed others to build for me.

In the process of getting unboxed I had to fall in love with everything about myself, and I mean all of me. I learned to forgive myself. I forgave my mother and my father for the secrets kept from me as a child. Secrets that I later learned about when I became an adult. I learned to teach people how to treat me. I made some radical changes in myself.

My husband and I were led to attend and serve at a non-denominational church. This was the first change. I prayed to have the courage to step out on faith. I gained the confidence to be present with myself. I learned to put me first. I practiced saying, "You are enough". I surrounded myself with people who celebrate me, and I celebrate them. I love to encourage, inspire, and empower women. I created a prayer corner in my house lined with prayers, scriptures, and my daily affirmations.

Finally, I surrendered it all to God, because the battle is the Lord's.

Latisha Lewis Price

Latisha

Latisha Lewis Price is a Mary Kay sales director, based in Gulfport, Miss. She holds a bachelor of arts degree in business administration and is a graduate of The University of Southern Mississippi. She worked for the Sun Herald newspaper in the Advertising/Marketing Department for 17 years.

She also worked in the corporate office of the YMCA, as a cake decorator at Delchamps, and in the business office at South Mississippi Regional Center. Working at SMRC, she learned to have compassion for people with disabilities; decorating cakes, she learned the color palette and precision; and at the YMCA, she learned that the community needs non-profit organizations.

She's married to Danny Price and has a bonus son, Danterrio Johnson.

CALL ME NAÏVE

By Angelyn Treutel Zeringue

"Pollyanna." "Rose Colored Glasses." "Glass always half full." These are some of the familiar phrases that come to mind when I describe my own perception of life. My story is not unique. Millions go through it. I have become a better person because of it all. As the first-born child to strong, loving parents, I was driven to be strong, pushed to achieve, encouraged to be nurturing, protective, and determined. I never thought I was particularly smart. All I knew was that something inside of me always compelled me to work hard, to do more than what was asked, and work to make others happy. I was the child who had good grades, won awards, and always helped those around me. I always look for the good in every situation.

Surprisingly, nothing in my story-book world ever worked out like I planned. Isn't that how life usually goes? I suppose that is the lesson in all of this. Each high and low in your life can be used to define you. Every aspect of your life provides you with the opportunity to choose – choose to be a better person from the experience or choose to give up. So, my story is about highs and lows and evolving. Always evolving....

After 13 years, I gave up a job that I absolutely loved! Having to move from a job you love, to helping in the family business can be devastating! However, it can also become the catalyst to bring about amazing opportunities in your life. For 13 years, I had been commuting 120 miles per day to a high-stress corporate job. I left home at 5:00 a.m. each morning and didn't get home until 6:00 p.m. to begin my mommy job of cooking, cleaning, homework, and more. I suffered from migraine headaches and back problems. On top of that I was a menace on the highway as I drove at crazy speeds and wrote notes in my notebook to keep from falling asleep. When I came into the family business, I nearly had a nervous breakdown from the change in pace and my loss of identity. The transition from the corporate world to a small-town family owned business was a huge adjustment! As I broke down in tears from the stress, a dear friend reminded me that I needed to become more introspective and put my life in God's hands. The Bible says, "Be still and know that I am God," Psalm 46:10. Be still?

I didn't even know how to do that. But I heeded the advice and began to try to stop – try to be still – and start to listen. In the quiet, you can hear God better. I decided to go where God would lead me. It was in the quietness that He led me to another place where I could thrive and serve others. He led me to become involved with the elementary school that my boys attended, and then I started volunteering for local community events. I began to bloom where I was planted. I threw myself into improving our community and developing young people. Just when I had settled into my new role, I experienced my next blow! It literally set me back! It blindsided me! It shook me to my very core! My marriage of 30 years ended. I felt betrayed and tossed aside. I retreated to the protective embrace of my faith, family and friends. It was now my chance to decide who Angelyn was and who she would be. I reflected on how I had always been someone's daughter, someone's mother, or someone's wife … but who was I? I had always done for others, and now I had to take time to decide what I wanted to be when I grew up. At this point, I could do what I wanted to do and be who I wanted to be. I was determined not to become an untrusting and bitter person due to my experience. I found myself becoming much more compassionate toward others going through heartache and relationship catastrophe. I had never imagined the depth of pain and despair that divorce could bring, until I experienced it for myself. The insight that I gained allowed me to become a better friend and sounding board for others. Through tragedy and triumph, I have discovered my inner strength. My mantra became "Keep moving forward; don't look back!" Even though I never thought it possible, my life became even more amazing.

I started my own business. I met a wonderful man who loves me more than I ever believed possible, and I thank God every day for the many blessings in my life. Honestly, if I had to do it all over again, I wouldn't change a thing. My life is rich and filled with faith, family, and friends. Maybe being naïve isn't so bad after all. And to you … as you're reading this, always remember: The best is yet to be!

Angelyn Treutel Leringue

Angelyn

Angelyn Treutel Zeringue, CPA, PWCAM, is a Trusted Choice independent insurance agent and president of SouthGroup Insurance Services - Gulf Coast and AST Solutions Inc. Treutel Zeringue is a prolific public speaker on technology, insurance and business issues.

She has been honored as Top Influencer, Volunteer of the Year, One Coast Top Community Leader, Person of Passion for Hancock County, Hancock County Citizen of the Year, National Top Women in Insurance, and America's Elite Women in Insurance. She tirelessly serves her community through Chamber of Commerce, Rotary International, American Heart Association, United Way, Leadership Programs and Women Entrepreneur groups.

REMEMBERING ME

By Angela Juzang

From an early age, I was sassy, bossy, and talkative. I knew exactly what I wanted and took deliberate, confident steps to get it. I moved through life with a certainty that made me feel like I could take on the world. From being captain of the cheerleading squad in the fourth grade to student body president my senior year in high school, I was thrust into many leadership roles. Some of which I chose, others which were chosen for me. Regardless, I became one of those "go to" individuals that people would turn to when they wanted to get something done. I was pegged as a rising star that was destined to achieve her full potential. Responsibility became an addiction. Being in the circle of influencers was the drug. I was living in a self-imposed cycle of doing what I thought others wanted me to do, versus identifying and focusing on what I wanted to do. The pressure to live up to other's expectations of me was enormous. I was mentally caged, but I didn't know that...yet.

By my early twenties, my life had changed drastically. This small-town-girl moved to the big city. I later understood it was my attempt to "find myself." In the meantime, what I found was my "Self" as a single mother, taking care of a newborn while enrolled in college full-time. Sometimes, I worked as many as two jobs to make ends meet, mainly retail, which meant long, sporadic hours. When I moved back to Gulfport, Mississippi after being away for more than a decade, my high school accomplishments felt like they had occurred in another lifetime. My self-esteem was in the dumps, because I thought I was a far cry from being the individual that was once voted "Most likely to succeed." At the time, I didn't realize that success would take on many forms throughout my life. To have survived my time in Atlanta as a member of the working-poor, using public transportation, and on government assistance, was a resounding success. To date, that time in my life was the hardest. Accepting it as an accomplishment, rather than a failure, was a huge step in breaking free. Free from trying to uphold an image that was imposed on me, by no one other than ... me.

It was strange to feel like a foreigner in a hometown that had once brought such promise. It was as if I had been on a long voyage and returned to find so many places, and people, changed. As I got my sea-legs back, I had to learn to make my way again in social circles. I had to build a professional profile that was indicative of my talents. My compass was simply a matter of remembering who I was, in spite of what had changed around me. This was a task that wasn't so simple.

It was during the process of making a career move from retail, to advertising sales (a business I knew nothing about) that would transform the way I approached new and different situations forever. During my interview, it was my prospective boss that first introduced me to the concept of transferrable skills. So that I would not be intimidated by my lack of specific industry knowledge, we identified outliers of my personality and professional abilities. We identified differentiating factors that would serve as a strong foundation upon which I could build within the company or (as I later found out), under any circumstance. Analyzing my experience and past pattern of behaviors, helped to predict my successes in the future and augmented my capabilities. Through the process we determined, I was a change-agent, thought-leader, self-motivated, and outspoken. I also demonstrated strong communication, organizational, and time-management skills. Above all else, I had a fearless ease with people that precipitated a comfort with selling, an ability that took some individuals years to establish. This resulted in a lucrative sales career. Over time, when I wanted to break into something new, or break free from something old, I called upon these fundamentals. These identified transferrable skills, were the essence of who I was. By relying on them, it became easier to trust myself, and to establish loyalty and influence with others.

Years later, when I was given yet another opportunity to change careers, (this time transitioning into the healthcare marketing field) I did so without hesitation, pushing through self-doubt, and accepting what I knew I could bring to the table. Sassy and confident, I embraced my life and all of the possibilities that came with it. I was now defining success on my terms, making it my choice, all while ... remembering me.

Angela Juzang

Angela

Angie Juzang was born and raised in Gulfport, Miss. Her professional career has included retail sales management with a national company, advertising sales for a television broadcast affiliate and marketing director at a facility that is part of the largest hospital corporation network in America. Her extensive business development experience has helped Angie create marketing solutions for small to large businesses, in addition to helping individuals build their personal and professional brand by connecting them through the establishment of various platforms, such The Legacy Group, and by hosting networking events to share relevant information and resources. Angie received her political science and Women's Studies bachelor of arts degree from Georgia State University in Atlanta, Ga.

She has received multiple community awards and accolades for being a thought-leader and change agent, working with organizations such as Boys & Girls Clubs, Mississippi Gulf Coast Chamber of Commerce, Leadership Gulf Coast, Goodwill and many more. She has one son, Tai, who is the light of her life.

CAN'T NEVER COULD

By Kathy Rogers

I refused to allow my lack of a college degree to define or box me in.

As a woman with only a high school diploma and a few college courses, combined with hard work and God's blessings, I believe I have accomplished a lot so far in life. My life hasn't been perfect but then whose is? My parents instilled a great work ethic in my sisters and me. My father was an electrician by trade and later became a tree removal expert. My father had no sons, so his three daughters became his helpers. He taught us how to work so we would be able to take care of ourselves. He always encouraged us to believe that we could be anything we wanted to. The words "I can't" were not allowed as an excuse! Rather, our motto was "can't never could" which translated means, you don't know that you "cannot" if you have never tried.

I believe that I can accomplish anything I want to until I am proven wrong; sometimes I have to be proven wrong more than once to be convinced I am in fact wrong. There have been times in my life that even though I was fully capable of doing a new job, I was looked down on and automatically disqualified because I did not have a college degree.

I graduated high school in May at age 17 and got married in June. I had two sons, Joseph, and Joshua, by age 20. By the age of 21, my former husband and I had started our own horse rental business, with 60 head of horses. By 1978. I was in the water well drilling business and co-owner of Lyman Well Company. I obtained my water well driller's license along with a water and wastewater operator's license. In the 1980s when I attended classes and went to job sites, I was usually the only woman. I also took care of the accounting side of the business.

In 1987, I experienced the trauma of divorce and got a job outside of the business that I owned. This is when I first discovered the value others put on a college degree and how my lack of a degree was viewed as a limitation by others. There were jobs for which I was qualified but could not apply because I did not have a degree. In order to be qualified for promotions, I began taking night classes in order to meet the educational requirements.

In 1991, I met and married my husband Lee. He proudly shared with me how much money he made. I promptly told him that his income would not feed beans to my boys. I made more money than he did, and he actually went to college. Fortunately, he responded positively and got down to business.

In 1994, we had our daughter, Annie. In 1996, I left my job at Stennis Space Center thinking I was going to be a stay at home mom. However, I found myself working with my husband. We bought some property, gutted and renovated the building and started Rogers Insurance; a property and casualty insurance agency. I obtained my P&C license in 1997; we also operated a financial services and life insurance business, Marston Rogers Group. In 2013, I obtained my life insurance license.

We had a great location and worked hard to build a reputation of integrity and great customer service. As a result, the 13th largest independent insurance agency group in the United States pursued us and solicited the purchase of our business. In 2016, we sold our P&C operations while retaining our financial services and life insurance business.

While I know from experience a college degree is not required to be successful in life; I also know for some careers they are a necessity. I encourage you to carefully examine the box you currently find yourself in. Decide if you are allowing this box to define who you are and what you will or will not be able to accomplish. Maybe this is your time to get free from your box and embrace who you were created to be! Remember, "can't never could."

Kathy Rogers

Kathy

Kathy Rogers is owner and vice president of Marston Rogers Group, a financial services and life insurance business. Having been a successful small business entrepreneur for 40 years her work experience is a versatile mix of knowledge and expertise in varying fields. As a life planner, her passion is to help individuals and businesses review where they are in life and business and help them design and implement life and retirement plans as well as business exit strategies.

Through proper planning and execution of these plans the financial anxiety surrounding life goals and retirement can be greatly reduced. She is co-founder and Board of Directors president of Adopt A Grandparent Day whose mission is to organize visits to seniors in nursing homes. She currently serves the Women's Resource Center as Board of Directors president, is a volunteer at Northwood Church, wife of Lee Rogers, mother of three and grandmother of five.

ABRACADABRA: UNBOXING MY VOICE
By LeKeisha Taylor Cotten

I was born in a box. In fact, my box was made from years of generational setbacks, hardships, and financial defeat that was the norm for my people. My mother was 14 years young when she gave birth to me; and despite all of my grandmother's efforts to will my mother's life in a different direction, the box my mother was born in eventually caved in on her. At the tender age of 24, my mother would succumb to heart failure. She never even tapped the surface of her potential.

For the next 15 years, I sat in a box of hurt, abandonment, depression and uncertainty, living in fear of dying the same death as my mother. I believed that I would not live past the age of 24. I was almost 30 years old before I realized that not only did I live past the age of 24, but my life kept on going. It was then, that I made the declaration that "I shall have what I say".

The Aramic phrase "Abracadabra," often used by magicians, means "I shall have what I say". When I came into the knowledge of how much power I possessed, I declared those words over my future. I can recall a time growing up when I would hear my grandmother praying to God, asking Him not to let both our water and lights get cut off at the same time. I can't recall a time when we actually did have both utilities disconnected at once – and my grandmother would in-turn thank God for answering her prayer.

When I think back, it brings me to tears knowing that she felt God had the capacity to only do one of those things. I had an abracadabra moment and declared that I would make things better. To think, I was a young teenage girl carrying this burden is insane. I would cry out "there must be something more to life than this!" Watching how my grandmother struggled gave me the drive to develop a prayer life that would ultimately shift the very path to my destiny.

I started writing. I wrote out visions – put pen to paper and even recordings of myself speaking things into existence. I had no idea as to how, when, or even IF, these things would come to pass. I simply knew that if I had vision and faith in God … abracadabra! After marrying and relocating to the Mississippi Gulf Coast in 2007, all things began to line up. I stepped out on a faith I didn't know I had, and many of those things I had written years ago started to show up!

I couldn't believe it! Was it really that simple? Could I truly have the things I say? Could I literally create my destiny by speaking? Everyday, I am reminded by a big resounding YES in my heart and spirit. My perspective on the power of words was transformed. I started to understand why my grandmother was so consistent and specific with her requests to the Lord. I understood that she possessed a power, within her capacity, to change the dynamic of our present situation.

I speak things into existence. When I get discouraged, I play back those old recordings of me speaking forth my success. I refuse to be lost in the growing crowd of people who are satisfied with never getting all that life has to offer. To every person reading the pages of this book, I challenge you to write out your vision, open your mouth and say, "abracadabra"! Lastly, believe that you can have what you say. Do the work! Burn the midnight oil! Wake up early to pray or meditate! Record yourself speaking to yourself. As awkward as it may feel, say your name out loud telling yourself what you are going to do to make it happen. More times than I can count, I wanted to call it quits, but I remembered my power to speak and free myself from the bondage of my mind. In a way, I am grateful for the box I came here in. For it was the confinement of the box, that forced out the fighter in me!

LeKeisha Taylor Cotten

LeKeisha

Award-winning recording artist and entrepreneur, LeKeisha Taylor Cotten, is a Mississippi Delta girl born in the city of Indianola. She is a product of humble beginnings, yet remarkably self-accomplished.

LeKeisha has traveled the world abroad singing, teaching, and ministering in both music and business. She is a licensed Christian minster and has shared the stage with countless greats. She is the founder of the Gulf Coast Gospel Music Awards, which has honored local and national individuals in the gospel and music industry.

LeKeisha is married to Curtis Cotten Jr., and they have two children, Mattie and Israel.

EMPLOYEE TO BUSINESS OWNER
By Marie A. Porter

I was raised in a day and time that people valued hard work. My parents believed that hard work paid off. They believed in doing the very best you could, no matter what you did. If you became a ditch digger, they believed you must become the very best ditch digger possible. They believed if you worked hard, you would be rewarded. My, how things have changed.

Working for a company you do not own is not always a negative thing. This is especially true if your superior allows you to run your department (or in my case your branch of the company) as if you owned it. If you are trusted and are treated as if you have a brain, you can certainly enjoy your job. However, working for a company that affords you these liberties can really spoil you. When my company was taken over by a government agency my world as I knew it, came to a screeching halt! All the blood, sweat and tears I gave meant nothing. No one cared that I worked 10-12-hour days, six days a week. I could no longer make decisions without someone else's approval. At this point I couldn't even supervise my staff appropriately.

After working in such a restricted environment, I was so ready for a change that I allowed another organization to talk me into coming to work for them. This was the very company that bought out my branch of the organization. Being that this was familiar territory, I assumed that I would be able to work the way I did before the government took over. I knew in my heart that this was not the right step for me, but I needed to be able to use my brain again. However, options are limited when you also need electricity, running water, food on the table and a roof over your head. I had excellent credit and I certainly didn't want to ruin that.

So, off I went to manage another branch of a financial institution where decisions were made by people higher up than you. Much higher up than you. I am talking about people who are making decisions from the ivory tower so to speak. They are so far removed from the real world that they make policies that have absolutely nothing to do with the real needs of the customer or day to day business. I had become a glorified babysitter. I could no longer take care of my customers the way I was accustomed. The process had completely changed from customer service, to process before people. I didn't even have the authority to make a loan for $1,000 without someone else's approval.

I was, indeed, BOXED IN. My intelligence and talents were in question. I felt like my talents no longer had any value. I no longer had the opportunity to use my brain for the good of the organization. They told me what I could and could not do. They even micromanaged how to perform my job and how to think. It was past time to break free! I could not survive and thrive in this box.

I worked for a savings and loan for about 20 years. I was a vice president and branch manager and I loved my job. I was respected for my intelligence, and my opinion was valued. I was able to take care of my customers and make personal loans and mortgages until the government took over because the commercial banks did not like us. It was an extremely difficult time. I never knew what it was like to be boxed in, until then. After working for the financial institution that bought my branch and customer accounts, I continued to feel limited and truly boxed in. After working for this organization for three years, I began looking for my opportunity to break free.

I never aspired to be a restaurant owner. After doing some extensive research into the Subway business, I took a leap of faith and purchased my first franchise. I had been managing people since I was 21 and I had helped others get loans to go into business for themselves. I knew I could do this. Once the decision was made, it was full steam ahead. Now remember my upbringing; I had to be the best at what I was doing. After building, buying, and selling I am the current owner of three Subway locations!

At 21, I really had no clue how to manage people. I had to learn that process over time. I am still learning, because each generation is different. I learned immediately that you must be present and talk to your staff to let them know that they are important to you. They will live up or down to your expectations. I learned to set expectations high and make them known right away. As a single mother for most of my adult life, I understand some of the hardships people go through. It is important to be able to relate to your staff on some level.

Knowing your true potential only comes when you have the opportunity to express your ideas and put them into action. If you are limited by the boundaries set for you by someone else, you will not blossom into your full self. Don't let someone else tell you what you can and cannot do.

Marie A. Porter

Marie

Born a Georgia peach, Marie moved with her family to Gulfport at age of 12. Marie is the mother of Lauren, a bilingual schoolteacher, and Michael, owner of a Subway franchise. She is the proud grandmother to three amazing young boys, ages 8, 3 and 2.

She is the proud owner and operator of three Subway franchises. Marie also serves as the chairperson for the local Subway owner's group, a position she has held for many years. As part of her volunteering, Marie serves as the treasurer for Pink Heart Funds, The Women's Club of Gulfport, the Mississippi Federation of Women's Clubs Southern District and she is the head of the finance committee at St. Peter's by-the-Sea Episcopal Church. In an effort to give back to the community, Marie serves on the "biscuit brigade" at her church which makes breakfast each Saturday for the homeless that gather at Feed My Sheep.

UNBOXING VISION
By Jocelyn Gavin Lane

There I was sitting on the table at the doctor's office scared out of my mind. I had found a lump and I was deathly afraid. My aunt is a two-time breast cancer survivor. As a child, I remember going with her to her chemotherapy treatments.

I never understood the long doctors' visits. My aunt was a determined woman. I can remember us riding in her Ford Probe from those long doctor visit when she was getting treatments. We stopped every 15 minutes so that she could vomit what seemed to be everything she had eaten that entire week. It's funny, the things you remember growing up. Apple green jolly ranchers were the only thing that soothed her on those long rides home. Those rides taught me patience and the importance of being selfless. After receiving the good news that I was cancer free, I decided that day, that I would do all the things I wanted to do. I would live my life unapologetically and unboxed. There were so many things I had aimlessly wandered through my life, "not doing." Thinking I wasn't good enough to be a lawyer in undergraduate school, kept me from even trying. I never applied to the nursing program because I just knew I wouldn't succeed if math was involved. I was a safe person. I wanted a good job with benefits and my goal was to work that job until retirement. Starting a business and an organization was in my mind, but far from anything I felt I could achieve on my own. Playing it safe, comforted my internal fears of rejection and my lack of self-value. It is often noted that rejection is one of our deepest human fears. What was I truly good at and how could I find that out? I was boxed in, but was it my fault? Had I become so rigid that I was on a path to nowhere?

We all scream insecurities are bad and we shouldn't feel insecure, but guess what? We all have them. The same goes for fear. We say that fear is bad, yet everyone faces fear in some way. What precisely are we so afraid of? Is it really failure? Is it the opinion of others? Better yet, what was I afraid of. Why hadn't I just gone for everything I thought I could do? I grew up in a family full of scholars. I mean straight A students with scholarships to Northwestern, Oberlin, Purdue, and Syracuse, William Carey, Alcorn, and DePaul. That's a lot to live up to. I was a pretty good student in high school, but I figured out quickly that I had to study. This was the first time I felt insecure about who I was, and I didn't want to fail. I wasn't sure if I wanted to go as far as New York, but I knew I wanted to succeed. However, failure was not an option, but fear can be crippling.

They say time heals all wounds. When you ask God to heal you from the crippling effects of fear, you must be ready. I asked for that in 2013 and I haven't looked back. I knew there were a few things I had a passion for, so I started there. I had a love for people- women and girls in particular. I wanted to bring about change that I felt was real and impactful. It was then that I started the Pink Lotus Project, a non-profit organization whose mission is to empower women and mentor girls. Pink Lotus Project is a beacon for local women who have a heart for service. I am honored to be at the helm, guiding the organization. In this same year, I started my business, Premier Professional Counseling Services, LLC. This was my vehicle to let my light shine as a mental health therapist. I wanted to give back to communities and help dismantle the stigma of mental health. I am a believer in helping others. Being true to who I am has helped me to be purposeful in my life.

My thinking was transformed when I realized that life is not all about us as individuals. Rather, it's what we can offer those around us. Remember, I had often thought about my talent and how I could manifest it. I started with my thought process. I had to start recognizing the self-defeating thoughts and cut them off early. I had to renew my mind and take the crucial steps to really do that. I would talk myself out of anything! I started to renew my relationship with God and commit myself to prayer. Not only for myself but those around me. I started to become intentional about what I wanted my life to look like and speak that into existence. I formulated goals, got some accountability partners, and started to take steps toward getting things done. I have made some mistakes along the way, but I keep moving forward .... unapologetically.

Through my own experiences I have learned some valuable lessons: I learned that women are more powerful than we think we are. We have to learn to give ourselves compassion and grace in challenging situations. Superwoman syndrome is real, and we have to do all we can to break that stigma. We are not superwomen; we are real women with emotions, fears, and breaking points. We need to adequately address our issues. When they can be addressed, we can truly break free and offer ourselves and someone else an apple green jolly rancher when it's needed.

Jocelyn Gavin Lane

Jocelyn

Jocelyn Gavin Lane is the owner and clinical director of Premier Professional Counseling Services, LLC. She is a graduate of Leadership Gulf Coast as well as graduate of the Department of Veterans Affairs Leadership Development Institute. She is the recipient of several awards: Spirit of the Ivy Award, Rose Mary Hayes Williams Humanitarian Award, Daughter of the Year award, Nora Graham Dreamer Award, and recognized as a Top Influencer at the 2018 Success Women's Conference.

She is the CEO and founder of The Pink Lotus Project a national nonprofit organization focused on empowering women and girls. She serves as a board member on several organizations on the Mississippi Gulf Coast.

Jocelyn and her family reside in Gulfport.

UNBOXING MY DREAMS

By Brandi Stage

My roots are in South Mississippi. Mom's family is from Louisiana and Dad's are from Mississippi. Mom remarried when I was young to a wonderful man. I'm blessed to have three parents that I love and adore.

My elementary years were spent in Southern Louisiana and some of my summers were spent on the Mississippi Gulf Coast. I guess you could say that I've always been a Mississippi girl. South Mississippi has a way of getting in your bones. No matter where I travel to, there is no place like home.

I married young and had two sons, Brandin and Tyler, who are now grown and amazing young men. After a long and difficult divorce, I raised my sons as a single mom for eight years. It was a difficult, adventurous and wonderful journey. In 2003, I remarried. The Lord gave me a husband, John, that was a blessing to all three of us. He raised my sons as if they were his own. We had many more adventures together and still do to this day.

Starting from a young age there were people in my life that tried to box me in. I remember even as a young girl, I would fight my way out if I could. I didn't like it when people would put limitations on me, whether it was friends or family. My Mom always taught me that I could do whatever I put my mind to, and I believed her. When someone would tell me I couldn't do something, it drove me to prove that I could. So, I did!

I remember when starting both of my businesses there was skepticism from those closest to me. Often the people closest to you can be the biggest skeptics. It becomes important to remember that the skeptics don't share the same vision, drive, and determination that you do. Often, they can be disguised as your biggest cheerleaders too! Don't hang your hat on the praise or the criticism of others. A word of caution here is to take wise counsel. Make sure you're asking experts in the areas that you are exploring and use discernment when discussing your plans with loved ones.

I specifically remember a time as an adult that I felt boxed in. I was definitely in the wrong career field. I had worked in three separate areas of this field. After the third area, I knew it just wasn't for me! I didn't feel like I could grow or spread my wings creatively. I also didn't feel like I could give my employers what they needed and deserved. The environment just wasn't conducive for my creativity! It felt as if I was drying up on the inside. However, it was the catalyst to rethinking my future and knowing that I wanted to work for myself again. Once again, I was met with skepticism from friends and family. However, they were only looking at aspects of starting a business from a place of fear. Once again, I knew I could do it ... so I did. After much research and finding a mentor in the beginning stages, my husband and I built a janitorial business together and never looked back.

Fast-forward several years later. I was driving down the road and the Lord spoke to me about doing photography as a business and not as a hobby anymore. John was completely on board, and I moved forward in my education and research. I graduated from the New York Institute of Photography. I had the opportunity to study under world-renowned photographers and created a portfolio that I loved and could market. It was so freeing!! Finally, I was free to spread my wings creatively!

A few years later, I remember being aware that I wasn't dreaming big enough. Because of my belief that "I could" I had realized many of my dreams and received the desires of my heart! I told my family that it was time for me to get new dreams and make these dreams — BIIIGGGGG ONES!! Once you set your mind on something:

Pray about it.

Keep it at the forefront of your mind.

Write it down.

Read it every day.

Take steps towards your goals and watch in amazement how things form.

It is important to know what your strengths are and to share them openly with others. You never know how this could be of help to someone. Always remember there is a place and purpose for you!

Let's talk confidence for a minute. Confidence is assurance. However, it's my opinion that self-confidence is fleeting. Don't get me wrong, working on yourself is a good thing, but it isn't what takes you to the highest form of confidence. It wasn't until I saw myself through Jesus' eyes that I became completely and utterly confident! There wasn't anything I had to do, (or could do for that matter) that could change how He saw me or how He made me! This revelation stripped away any fear of what people thought of me. Now that kind of confidence is everlasting!

What about the limitations we set for ourselves? Ever thought about boxing yourself in? It's scary to take leaps of faith, but it can also be freeing and exhilarating. If you're wanting to start a business, do your research, talk to experts and pray, pray, pray. If you're wanting to make a change in your life, rinse and repeat! But for goodness sake, break free! Imagine what you could do or accomplish if there were no limitations! Just imagine!!

Brandi Stage

Brandi

Brandi Stage is a graduate of the New York Institute of Photography. Her work has been featured on the covers of Gulf Coast Woman magazine. She's active in the community, serving on the Board for the Women's Resource Center in Gulfport, member of PPLA, GCN, CTE, SBE, and Gulf Coast Chamber of Commerce.

Brandi Stage is a portrait photographer who creates an exceptional magazine-style photoshoot experience for everyday people as well as dynamic and stunning images for individuals, families, and professionals.

Brandi lives on the Mississippi Gulf Coast with her husband and children.

TO BE OR NOT TO BE-ME

By Cecelia Shabazz

I don't necessarily know when it happened. If it was forced on me, or if in some way I permitted it. I was hiding behind masks of various emotions. I was smiling when I wanted to shout and sitting back when I wanted to stand up. These moments saturated my heart with insecurities that threatened to shape me. All of this occurred from succumbing to countless requests, demands, and expectations placed on me by others. The demands were both implicit and explicit. Either way, I was giving in or putting myself in a position to become someone I wasn't. Without intention, I had become "boxed."

As I look back over my life, I can piece together how it took root. Many people have said that I am too sympathetic, too encouraging, too passionate, too optimistic, and too nice. However, my perspective was that it takes all types of people to connect to others. What I once saw as my strengths, were responsible for building the walls to my box. Eventually, it felt like the qualities that were so intricate to my personality had somehow become this virus that was injected into my DNA.
I felt that in order to succeed in my career, in leadership, and in life I needed others to define who I was.

They said, "Cece, you have to change if you want to be effective." But change what? I asked myself. If I can't be me then who exactly am I? What is my value? These feelings began to silence me. They began to steal my confidence. I began to feel that in some way my personality is what made me inadequate.

With all these feelings of self- doubt and insecurity about who I was ... another wall of the box goes up. How did I get here?

These verbal assaults started to eclipse my very nature. I remember trying to mimic what a "successful" person acted like to make others feel comfortable and confident in me. At this point, it felt like I had given away my influence and power. I began to feel powerless! Somehow, I needed to take that power back! I needed to become unboxed! In order to think outside of this box, I had to understand it first. I began to analyze the situation. I came to realize that every box can be opened! The very purpose of a box is to store things inside until needed. All of those frustrating moments that crafted my box gave me the opportunity to evaluate all of my innate qualities.

This process exposed all my strengths and weaknesses. I learned to explore them. I learned to evaluate them and appreciate them. I learned to play them to my advantage. Finally, I gave myself permission to explore who I was. I gave myself the freedom to engage in new behaviors. This process helped me set myself apart within my industry. It allowed me to foster a personal brand that gives me opportunities such as this one, as well as manage expectations. I'm a better leader now because of it. I have learned how to meet people where they are, while respecting and encouraging their innate qualities.

My mom once told me to shine! She said that I was created like the sun and my assignment was to bring light to dark places. I believe her words. When I walk into a room, I totally believe I change the atmosphere. I believe that I bring value to all my relationships. I believe I make a difference, just as I am.

I love this quote by author, Marianne Williamson because it resonates with me. She says, "Our deepest fear is not that we are inadequate. Our deepest fear is that we are powerful beyond measure. It is our light, not our darkness that most frightens us. We ask ourselves, who am I to be brilliant, gorgeous, talented, and fabulous? Actually, who are you not to be? You are a child of God. You're playing small does not serve the world. There is nothing enlightening about shrinking so that other people won't feel insecure around you. We are all meant to shine, as children do. We were born to make manifest the glory of God that is within us. It's not just in some of us; it's in everyone. As we let our own light shine, we unconsciously give other people permission to do the same. As we are liberated from our own fear, our presence automatically liberates others."

This inspiring quote is a reminder that each of us is purposely designed and have an inherent right to be who we are. It's our God-given superpower! As Psalm 139:14 beautifully states, "I praise you (God) because I am fearfully and wonderfully made; your works are wonderful, I know that full well." Give yourself the opportunity to know the same.

Cecelia Shabazz

Cecelia

Cecelia is an award-winning creative director and graphic designer, named 2013 and 2014 Creative Director of the Year and 2016 Silver Medal recipient for Excellence in Advertising by the Mississippi Gulf Coast chapter of the American Advertising Federation.

She has more than 18 years of experience crafting dynamic design in print and web. Cecelia holds a bachelor of fine arts in graphic communications from The University of Southern Mississippi and is an adjunct instructor at both University of Southern Mississippi and Tulane University, teaching courses in media arts

When Cecelia is not working, she is volunteering her time in ministry and community events.

Cecelia lives in Gulfport, Miss., with her husband, Gabriel.

FINALLY FREE

By Dawn Lieck

Getting "unboxed" is not always a one-step move, it's an ongoing journey. A journey of continually traveling to your eternal "why."

In embracing our why, we sometimes mistake it with a singular motivation, but the two couldn't be more different. You must first get to the core of what you truly want for yourself. In embracing our why, we sometimes mistake it as a singular action which is far from true. In order to accomplish the goal of finding your why you must go through many layers to reach your that goal which requires multiple actions ... .

Let me explain. I knew I was miserable in my six-figure job and my 20 year. marriage. They were both interconnected. If I left the marriage, I'd still be working 70-80 hours a week. If I left the job and stayed in the marriage, that would create even more anxiety and upheaval in my life. Together they both had created the ultimate trap. How do you leave a high paying job that a marriage won't survive or leave a marriage with no money? How could I ever escape these chains and survive?

It took a very strategic plan and an entire year, but I did it! I made it! I was "unboxed." A huge accomplishment. Now I was on my own. I obviously needed income so I got a new job that paid less money, but without the stress and responsibility. I was living the dream! Or was I?

You see I had unboxed myself from the unhappy marriage and the upper management high-stress job, but, what I had actually done was "reboxed" myself. I had taken another job that dictated what I did workwise and dictated what I did with my time. I was boxed ... AGAIN.

When the feelings of being trapped resurfaced, I thought "what have I done?" I had to revisit my "why." The deep down "why."

My why is Freedom. I want to be the sole decision maker for everything in my life. I cannot have any aspect of it dictated by others in order for me to be truly happy and content. Your "why" must be constant. Your "why" must be included in your every move and decision.

You must ask the question: Is this decision conducive to my "why"? If not, regroup! I now choose to utilize my "job" as my silent investor for my "why." I work to allow myself to invest in my dream, my business, my "why," which is FREEDOM.

When I made my first plan to come out of my marriage and job, I did so under the pretense that I was miserable. They no longer served me or my overall happiness. In all actuality I hadn't identified the true reason for my unhappiness, I just knew I wasn't happy. In order for me to change that, I knew it would require some huge life-changing decisions. I went for it! All of it! I don't regret a second of it!

Looking back, I wish I had identified the core issue first. Maybe if I had, I wouldn't have spent four years in a different box! Again, I say, becoming unboxed isn't always a one time move – it's a journey.

In the process, make sure you're focusing on your eternal "why." Don't just focus on that singular goal, like losing weight or changing jobs. Don't get me wrong, those are valiant accomplishments.

However, if you still haven't identified the core issue within yourself, the feeling of success will soon disappear, and you'll find yourself back at square one!

The following steps will help you begin your journey to finding your eternal why:

1. Dig deep – What is the reason you're unhappy? What is boxing you in? Why do you feel that way? What is the ultimate outcome? How do you want to feel? (Remember, no singular goals!)

2. What steps do you need to take to start your journey of unboxing? What does it look like? These steps must be intentional. They must only be steps that will ensure progress towards your eternal "why."

3. Write your plan. Plans made only in our heads will be changed when the journey becomes uncomfortable. Pushing through the discomfort is the only way to the other side.

4. Revisit your written plan over and over again. Is this decision going to get me to my desired outcome? Don't mistake activity for productivity. Being busy does not mean you are making headway to progress. Remember the prize. That prize is YOU!

I did not become "unboxed" without an immense amount of fear. Much to the contrary, I was terrified! There were times in my journey that I was positive I wouldn't make it. The negative self-talk would step in and try to take control. My critics told me I was being unreasonable; I was not being realistic.

Who makes such drastic changes in their forties? This girl, that's who. My eternal "why" was my driving force, I had to be free. Free to be myself, free to love myself, free to put myself first for the first time in life instead of continually disregarding my own feelings.

If you allow irrational fear to control you, it will debilitate you, along with every opportunity to become unboxed. Fear can bind you as tight as chains. It will cause you to remain in that box.

Is your eternal "why" strong enough to overcome the fear? If you've soul searched well enough, it absolutely is. Being intentional and making yourself your top priority will ensure your success. There's only one way to become unboxed. That way is through you!

Bet you didn't know you've held the box cutter all along...

Dawn Lieck

Dawn

Dawn Lieck is a bold out-of-the-box health and wellness life coach, author, transformation speaker and CEO of Finally Free, LLC. Dawn is transforming lives of tenacious women who desire to thrive in self-discovery and development. She is intentional about impacting women's lifestyles with providing them the tools to pursue their inner most dreams emotionally, physically and mentally.

Dawn has graced the stage with award-winning, international speaker Cheryl Wood, hosted incredible empowerment luncheons, Co-authored "Women Inspiring Nations 2", co-chaired of one of top national women's in business conferences (Success Women's Conference) and is a member of Leadership Gulf Coast Class, Board of Directors of Lighthouse @ Business and Professional Women.

NO LIMITS

By Kerri Paul

My friends and family thought I was crazy.

It's been a common theme in my life, as I have frequently made decisions based upon self-reflection and manifestation. Growing up in the 90s shaped who I am as an adult. We were told we could be anything, do anything, put our mind towards a goal, and get it done. "Can't never could and won't never would" is a phrase that reverberated from my third-grade teacher's tongue, and I, typical type A Millennial, believed it.

Mompreneur is a neologism to describe the lifestyle that I ascended to, or rather, the lifestyle that God chose for me. I always knew that I wanted to work for myself and make my own decisions as a boss and a mother. But I had no idca the types of "boss-like" decisions that lay ahead for me in motherhood.

In my 30s, I was a college-educated, professional working in corporate America. My husband was walking in his purpose, having played professional sports, and then working in his career in Major League Baseball. We had it all. We built a life for ourselves that fit, and we thought we were unstoppable. What we wanted, we worked hard to achieve, and crushed goals one by one. After building our dream home and settling into the neighborhood that we had been crushing on for some time, our married life came to a crossroads. We wanted and moreso, "needed" more in our life. We were 30-somethings in the prime of our life, and it was time for a new chapter, parenthood.

After trying unsuccessfully for about a year, we turned to fertility enhancements. Soon enough we received the news that we had desperately been anticipating that we were expecting. I like to consider myself in-tune with my body, and something seemed different with the pregnancy. It felt as if my body was growing at a much more rapid pace than my other family members at this stage of their pregnancies. Also, my symptoms were, let's say, "enhanced." It didn't take long for me to surmise that God had granted us a double dose of blessings, and the feeling was confirmed upon my first official ultrasound appointment. And then there were two!

I always envisioned my opportunity to bring life into this world as a natural process. I recalled the sitcom moms with their Lamaze "whoo-whoo-hee-hee" breathing techniques and dreamed of a natural childbirth experience for myself. I shared my desire to deliver naturally with my friends, family, and co-workers. And likewise, they all thought I was crazy. "That's what they make an epidural for!" "There's no way you will be able to deliver twins naturally!" "Twins? No way!" The doubt came in from every which way, but I did my best to reaffirm to myself "You CAN!"

I started searching my area for any information on natural childbirth, and unsurprisingly, I came up short. There is a true crisis of maternal healthcare support, especially in the south and for women of color, as I found very little resources on natural childbirth. It was as if I was speaking a different language. Not many around me understood the concept of elective natural labor, especially with the delivery of two babies. Was there truly no support for me to bring my twins into the world naturally, the way that God intended? At that point, self-doubt began to creep in. Naturally, I looked to my inner circle for support. Even in speaking with my closest friends about my desire to deliver my babies naturally, they sympathized to my wants, but they were even unsure of which direction to point me. Natural childbirth simply wasn't "a thing" that we had been exposed to, for one reason or another. Looking back, I was one of the earlier females in my circle to start a family, so we weren't privy to pregnancy and motherhood information. We were all DINKS (double income-no kids) aspiring to climb the corporate ladder at that time. I wasn't intimately acquainted with anyone who had elected a natural childbirth. Alternately, my personal experience with those who had delivered by Cesarean was daunting. Each of those pregnancies and births were high-risk, included long term bed rest, and even a few ended with emergency surgery to save the lives of both the mother and the baby. To say that I was traumatized by even the mention of major surgery to deliver my babies was an understatement.

How would I break through society's new version of childbirth? How would I "unbox" myself from the new "norm" of indoctrinating women to feel uncomfortable with our bodies, not to trust ourselves, and to fear the birth experience? I was left to rely on my own inherent beliefs and principles. I rested on the knowledge that I am woman! Through my faith in God and in my own self, I knew that I was fearfully and wonderfully made, literally, as a vessel by which to bring life into the world. The pregnant me felt more like a woman than I had ever in my life. My blood intermingled with that of my two precious babies who were growing inside of my womb, and hormones surged. We were connected, though I was mentally disconnected by the anguish and fear of unknowing.

Thankfully, prayer, manifestation, and research brought me to discover the Bradley Method, as I was introduced by one of my colleagues to a doula in Hattiesburg, Miss., who taught the life-affirming doctrine. The husband-coached childbirth method utilizes a holistic, natural, and family-centered approach where the husband and wife focus, together, on prenatal education, nutrition, exercise, and relaxation for a healthy and natural birth.

Now, when I say that we trained for our moment, we wholeheartedly trained for the marathon that is natural childbirth. I exercised with my personal trainer and kept a nutrition log of my foods. In the South, pregnant bellies in the gym are quite the sight, but I carried all three of us to my weekly workout sessions to strengthen my body and mind.

Nightly, my husband and I studied and prayed together for a safe and healthy delivery. We even practiced pain toleration techniques to help prepare for and relax through the pain. Most importantly, the documentation of our goals and needs in a birth plan helped us to visualize and strategically plan for our day to cross the threshold of parenthood. Not many around us understood what we were doing and again, many of the folks around us thought we were crazy. But another person's opinion of me was none of my business!

Well prepared, I carried my twins to 37.5 weeks, and they made their way into the world naturally, with no complications, and the way the God (and mommy) intended. As a both a businesswoman and a mother, I credit my natural childbirth experience as my most precious and proud accomplishment in my life. It's difficult to explain succinctly, but the experience, from pregnancy to birth, is one in which I felt most whole as a woman, centered, and empowered as a person. In labor, I was in my most vulnerable yet strongest position as a woman, as through the endurance of pain, God provided the most precious gifts.

As a mother and a woman in business, keeping it all together is quite the balancing act. There is always pressure to melt into the status quo and place limits upon our own reach for greatness. Like the path that many women choose for childbirth, they seek to numb the pain of life's natural experiences. I, on the other hand, desire to live presently in my moments. I revel in the exhilaration, the burn, the climax and denouement of every experience that God places in my path. How are we to truly understand and capture life's greatest pleasures of love, success, and happiness if we are numb to their opposites in anguish, challenges, and pain?

As women, we must put a stop to limiting ourselves and living within the fence that society has built around our minds. I implore women to reach deep inside of themselves when making decisions that affect their ascent to greatness. We can no longer allow other's doubts and reservations creep into our heads and poison our passions. Be fearless! There's nothing to fear but fear itself. I have learned the credence in goal setting, education, and manifestation, and have built my life's empire around utilizing these tenets for success. Women can either be held hostage by other's thoughts and visions for themselves or they can unbox the eagle and fly. I choose the latter, and I pray that we teach our sisters and daughters to break free and soar.

Kerri Paul

Kerri

Kerri Paul, mompreneur, juggles three toddlers (a set of boy/girl twins with baby sister trailing right behind) along with a burgeoning career as a restaurateur on the Mississippi Gulf Coast. She and her husband, Matt, brought the trendy-yet-casual brunch restaurant franchise Brick & Spoon, to the Mississippi Gulf Coast in 2019, and continue to work building and marketing the brand along the Southeast.

An influential businesswoman, Kerri is sought after for her insight and creativity in motherhood, entrepreneurship, hair, and beauty. The self-coined, spirited "Opinionista" enjoys contributing her 10 cents as a Mombassador and blogger on the lifestyle and parenting site Mommination.com. Fun Fact: she competed on Season 20 of CBS' Emmy-winning competition reality show The Amazing Race.

NO LONGER UNWORTHY
By Sherry Moxley Seaman

Growing up, I was very blessed to be raised by God-fearing, loving and hard-working parents. They did their best to give me a good Christian upbringing. My parents had a tender marriage, and while I'm sure it was not perfect and they had difficult moments, it was never expressed in front of me and my siblings.

Naturally, I imagined I would marry and enjoy my own happily ever after. Like so many people, I tried to live up to a standard because I didn't want to disappoint anyone, especially my family. Well, that's exactly what I did, and that's how I became boxed in. Without realizing it, I allowed the fear of what others thought or would think of my actions to begin to shape my future.

I was married at 17, had a baby by 21, and was divorced at 23. I was told that if I divorced outside of what the Bible teaches, I had a one-way ticket to hell. Yikes! I'm sure this came from people who meant well and offered it as correction, but I took it to another level. I felt I was being judged and had a mark on my life that could never be erased. As a result, I was constantly in a place of self-examination and feeling unworthy, not good enough.

For years, I felt my family, church friends and pastors all viewed me as the "bad child" and "the girl with the past" who would forever be lost. I don't know how true this was, but it became real to me that they saw me this way. Perception is reality, right? Because I viewed this as judgment, it led me down a path of self-destruction. A string of bad choices just chiseled away at my sense of self-worth.

I was still on the hunt for love. Several years and several relationships later, I met a charismatic, handsome guy who swept me off my feet. We eventually married and he spoiled and showered me with love and affection, built up my self-esteem and helped me build a six-figure income in direct sales. But more importantly, he loved and raised my son as if he were his own. I thought I had finally got it right and was living my fairytale lifestyle. For 13 years, life was perfect — or so I thought.

Eventually, his world began to unravel all around me. I remember the day I opened two certified letters; one from the U.S. Immigration Office and one from a bank. Imagine my shock to learn he had felony charges against him and was not eligible for citizenship. It got worse, and eventually, I found myself with over $90,000 in debt I didn't create. I was hurt, mad, disappointed and, of course, it didn't take long for me to start wearing, "FAILURE" as a badge again.

I decided it was time for all work and no play. In my mind, I felt if love can't fill me, success will, right? I chased a title and felt validated by my success. I finally realized that the cars, diamonds, large checks, fancy homes, awards, and plaques would never erase the mark I felt was upon my life.

I couldn't figure out how to live and forgive myself and I desperately wanted to erase all the mistakes and disappointments, but I couldn't. The baggage I carried kept me boxed in.

After catching up with an old friend of 20 years, he offered me a position as vice president in his advertising agency. He encouraged me, as well as others and eventually, I began to reclaim my self-esteem, but I still felt incomplete. I eventually had a light-bulb moment and realized it's not about finding the right person to be with, it is about you becoming the right person.

That was the beginning of me climbing out of that box that contained me. After a lot of self-reflecting and a lot of praying asking God to help me to forgive myself, I saw a shift. I stopped making poor decisions when it came to relationships. I started to care less about what others thought about me and stopped being worried if they were judging me.

I began to trust the Lord and asked Him to direct my steps.

I finally realized that after a life of trial and errors, all I ever really needed was Jesus. He loves me and that helps me love myself. I'm in the midst of living my best life now, enjoying every minute being the wife, the daughter, the sister, the mother, and now a Glammie, that I was meant to be. The ability to forgive myself and realize I'm good enough has led me to find the right person, my husband Steve after I became the right person. Now, I pray I can inspire other women to be loving and accepting of themselves

Sherry Moxley Seaman

Sherry

Sherry is from Augusta, Ga., and now lives in Biloxi, Miss. For 30-plus years, she has been a marketing consultant in media and currently serves as director of business development for Gulf Coast Woman magazine. For 23 of those 30 years, she built a successful business in a direct sales/network marketing company, where she earned 12 cars (four of those pink Cadillacs), diamond rings, and much more.

Sherry has led women all over the U.S. to become six-figure income earners. She has received countless honors, awards and recognition, but none more than being a mother and "Glamma".

FREE YOUR MIND
By Jemina Ballard

It all happened on a Monday when the color of the day was cloudy blue instead of sunny yellow. I woke up that morning and immediately grabbed my forehead, trying to stop the pain of a throbbing migraine. If you've had one before, then you know the physical feeling of being trapped inside your own head with no way of escape. All I wanted to do was pull it out! Of course, you can't just pull out a physical ailment, nor can you snap your fingers and make it go away. So off to work I went with my hair in a tight ponytail, which was making the migraine worse. At the time, I didn't realize that the tightness of the ponytail was contributing to the pain.

At the end of the day, I took the ponytail down and left my hair out. The moment I took the band off, the freedom my head felt was indescribable! At that moment, I forgot about the pain and embraced the pressure release. Although it was my hair that was tied up, I realized that when your head isn't free, nothing else will be. In order to be free within ourselves, we have to be free in our mind first. When the mind is tied up with thoughts of bondage, nothing can be done to build it up.

This brings one to a mental breakdown. Letting my hair be free was symbolic of how our lives are at times. There are ideas and purposes within us that are waiting to come out, but this can only happen when we release what's tying us up.

We must also be aware of who and what we are connected to. What we are linked to can cause a "chain reaction." For example, when we are mentally linked to fear, it can lead to doubt. When we are emotionally linked to worry, it can lead to stress. It's imperative to break those chains and link to freedom, leading to joy, and peace. It's what's on the inside of you that is working on the outside of you, to show what you are made of.

When a bodybuilder goes to the gym to exercise, one of the things they may do is "lift weights." Having the capacity to lift the necessary weight takes strength, courage, and physical ability. Bodybuilders keep going even though the more they lift, the heavier things become. I say this because as women, God literally created you to be the carrier of weight. Not only do you have the capacity, but you also have a built-in ability.

This is why the woman was chosen to become pregnant and carry the weight of her unborn child for nine months. Every time you feel weighed down spiritually, be reminded that God has formed you to stay lifted up. See it as a privilege that you were equipped for the task, physically and emotionally ... even when it's uncomfortable at times.

Your feet may get tired, your emotions may fly off the handle and your back may begin to hurt, but know who has your back (God), and He won't let it break. At the end of every day, it's in Him that you WILL find much rest after you have given your all. So, get up, weigh in and keep going in this journey of life. God has equipped you to handle the weight! He is able to give you night vision in dark places, so never let anything cause you to become blindsided. How you see things from your perception will be based on your point of view.

You were meant to be free. If there are things that are binding you up, let them go. The moment you do, you will be and feel free. Don't let anything tie you in a knot. Let your "hair" (figuratively speaking) down and remain free!

Jemina Ballard

Jemina

Jemina works for the United States Air Force as a civilian human resources specialist. She is the minister and founder of the Daughters of Faith International Women's ministry. She holds a bachelor of science degree in hospitality management from the University of Southern Mississippi, Hattiesburg.

Daughters of Faith serves in the community, helping the unfortunate by giving them hope through giving. Jemina has been hosting shoe giveaways since 2013, collecting more than 1,000 shoes. In 2015 and 2016, Jemina hosted a project called "She Survived," where she along with women in the community collected more than $2,000 worth of daily needed personal items and donated them to a women's shelter.

As Jemina is instructed by God, her vision for this group is to change the culture of women in her community by helping women realize they can do all things through the one that made them who they are, Jesus the Christ.

THE ICE-BREAKER EYE-OPENER

By Ellis Anderson

As an ice-breaker, our hostess at a gathering of women tossed out a question. "What degrees do you hold?" she asked when we sat down for dinner.

A retired college professor, she'd probably played the little get-acquainted game at some academic conference and thought it would help put us all at ease. She had no reason to think any of us might be made uncomfortable by the question. The women who sat around that table back in 2004 were professionals, business owners and educators from the Mississippi Gulf Coast and New Orleans. All of us were in the prime of our careers and like me, middle-aged. Of course, we all had college degrees.

At the far end of the table, I was last in line and glad of it. I reached for my wine glass and took a big swallow.

To get things started, our hostess began. According to my recollection of the evening, she reeled off several college degrees she held, with Ph.D. being the penultimate. She wasn't bragging. She was simply explaining her very interesting and satisfying career path.

The question slowly made its way around the table toward me, with lots of laughter and questions following each answer. A few others held doctorates. At the bare minimum, all of the women had graduated with a bachelor's degree and gone on to get a master's. Everyone in the room held at least two college degrees.

I tried to calm my anxieties. After all, I had nothing to be ashamed of. Still, I hoped they'd drink enough wine to get sidetracked before they got to me. However, luck was not in my corner. When it was finally my turn, I took a breath. At that moment, I decided that a few colorful details might make the answer seem more interesting than disgraceful.

"Me?" I said. "I was a National Merit Scholar with three months to go when I came to New Orleans for spring break. That was 1978. I ended up dropping out of college. I moved to the French Quarter and became a street musician."

No one said a word.

"I don't have any degree," I said, throwing out my arms in a joking ta-da gesture.

The eyes of those who didn't know me well – including our hostess – widened. My friends in the room laughed. Then all the women hastened to reassure me that there was no judgment attached, that degrees didn't make the person. But the hostess couldn't let it go.

"Why didn't you finish later?" she asked, incredulous.

I explained that since I'd attended an evangelical college, my transcript was heavy on religious classes. Many of the credits wouldn't transfer. When I applied to schools in New Orleans, they would accept me, however, I'd have to start over as a sophomore. I wasn't inclined to give up another three years of my life and go into debt to get a B.A.

To give a little feel-good closure to the game, I insisted to the women that lack of a degree had never prevented me from anything I wanted to do.

Until that night, I'd believed that. But the next day, the discomfort I had felt at that dinner party forced me to start re-examining my tightly constructed box of beliefs. Had dropping out of college hamstrung my self-confidence in subtle ways, undermining me in ways I'd denied?

Of course, I understood that millions of extremely successful and well-rounded people never attended college. In fact, most of my own immediate family didn't have college degrees – I would have been the first, had I not dropped out.

For the first time, I began to confront my status as a "drop-out" head-on. Over the following weeks, I kept circling back to what my dad repeatedly told me as I was growing up. He said a college degree isn't so much about what you learn in classes; it just proves to others - and yourself - that you have the gumption to undertake a big project and follow it through to completion.

My father was neither a drop-out nor a graduate. He'd never had the opportunity to attend college at all. Although he'd excelled at a prestigious private high school and was on the fast-track for an equally prestigious university, his foster parents – who had brought him home from an orphanage when he was only a toddler - died suddenly when he was 16. Orphaned for a second time, my dad was thrust back into the state foster care system and forced to leave his high school.

My mother's side of the family went back to the 1700s in deep Appalachia. Hard-scrabble subsistence farmers, they were never prosperous, and the Great Depression hit them hard. College was thought of as a luxury for rich city people down in the lowlands. My mother, with the help of family friends, left the mountains when she was 18 and attended secretarial school in Richmond in 1939. That achievement was a lifelong source of pride to her.

Looking back at my parents' histories, I began to realize the bitter disappointment they must have felt when I abruptly left college. Yet, they were amazingly good sports considering the circumstances. While they had occasionally encouraged me to go back, they had never berated my decision to quit.

Once I'd unboxed my rigid perspective in my late 40s, I began to look into the possibility of entering college again. However, I found the rules hadn't changed. My twenty-year-old credits would only grant me sophomore status. I couldn't see giving up my full-time business for three years and incurring student debt for an undergrad degree - even though obtaining one now had new importance.

Then, in 2013, an old college friend told me that our university had begun offering online classes. I met with advisors there who configured my curriculum. After nine months of challenging online classes, I finally graduated – 36 years later than planned.

The only disappointment? My parents had already passed away. The expected benefits? Something deep within me shifted and seemed to click into place. My self-confidence may still get weak knees at times, but my inner footing stands steady on that concrete foundation.

The surprise outcome? I found I thrive on the educational process. I'm currently enrolled in an MFA program for Creative Writing at the University of New Orleans, where I'm working on the manuscript for a second book. My business workload only allows me to take one class a semester. Admittedly, even that sometimes feels overwhelming.

But now I've got the gumption to see me through.

Ellis Anderson

Ellis

Ellis Anderson has 25 years' experience in creating and implementing community-building concepts. Major projects include event planning, video production, community outreach and awareness campaigns, and publication of ground-breaking blogs and online magazines, like The Shoofly Magazine and French Quarter Journal (launching July 2019).

Her book about a community faced with unimaginable challenges – "Under Surge, Under Siege, the Odyssey of Bay St. Louis and Katrina" – was published by University Press of Mississippi and won the 2010 Eudora Welty Book Prize and the Mississippi Library Association Non-Fiction Author's Award.

REJECT THE RESIDUE
By Tanya Marie Lewis

I was blessed to grow up in a home saturated with love. I was 9 years old when I realized that the love my Mama had in her heart toward us was not the norm. It was as if I had been living in a cocoon, but that couldn't shield us from a real world out there with some unhealthy and unhappy people.

I was in the second grade when Mama purchased her first home in a very beautiful neighborhood on the other side of town. My excitement of starting a new school was met with much opposition that I didn't expect, nor did I understand at the time. There was this one teacher, let's just call her Ms. Penny, who looked like me. I wanted to grow up to be a teacher, too, so I couldn't wait to become one of her students and glean from her.

My dream of her taking me under her wings was not in the plans. This woman apparently hated me and seemed to go out of her way to embarrass me every chance she got. The first time it happened, my class was standing in line waiting to go into the library. She pulled me out of line and stood me in front of the entire class and nitpicked everything about me, from my hair, to my clothes, all the way down to my shoes. While the students laughed, I cried, which only made the situation worse because she started calling me a cry baby. Her abusive behavior gave permission to the students to bully me. The abuse continued, and what started out with simple things like pulling ribbons out of my hair turned to shoving me in the back, tripping me, hitting me in the head, taking my lunch every day and threats of violence.

It got so bad that I started making excuses not to go to school (which I loved) and it worked for a little while until Mama kept asking questions. I finally had to tell her what was going on. She immediately went up to the school and I'm not sure what she said or who she talked to, but Ms. Penny settled down. She still did little things on the side, but they were very subtle as not to draw attention. I'm not sure what would have happened had my Mama not intervened when she did because I had contemplated suicide because of the torment I was experiencing.

I remember my Mama telling me, "Tanya, there are people who will hate you just because of the favor of God on your life. Don't forfeit anything God has for you because someone else doesn't think you deserve it."

I moved on from Ms. Penny, but the residue of her abuse followed me well into my adulthood. You see, I met the spirit of Ms. Penny repeatedly in the form of other people, but with age, and lots of prayers I've learned how to break the cycle of abuse when I see it rear its ugly head.

The Ms. Pennys of this world can be our greatest asset or worse liability. You see, this woman had the chance to make a difference. She had great influence in my life and instead of nurturing me, she abused me because of her own insecurities. She boxed me into self-hatred, low self-esteem, and all the things that kept me stagnant for many years of my life.

Ms. Penny had projected her issues on me. It's often the projections of others that keep us boxed in. I think when we take the time to reflect back on our life, we'll realize that a single incident that occurred early on has left a stain. That stain can create negative patterns in our life that linger for years. We find ourselves dealing with the same struggles over and over.

Something powerful happens once you realize you don't have to subscribe to another person's perception of you.

This realization is what helped me to become unboxed from words spoken over me and the residue of abuse perpetrated against me.

It's time for you to get out of the box that has been holding you back, too. Romans 8:28 reminds us, "And we know that all things work together for good to them that love God, to them who are the called according to his purpose."

Get out the box. Stay out the box. Reach into your purpose, grab hold of it and soar!

Tanya Marie Lewis

Tanya

Tanya Marie Lewis is on a mission to see God's women embrace their worth in Him so that they can function in the marketplace without fear or anxiety in doing what He has commissioned them to do. She is a lover of Jesus, family, people, coffee, and author of several books. She owns Birth The Vision Publishing and Consulting and is editor of Handmaidens in the Marketplace magazine.

She is the editorial director of The Notes Anthology project, a book series that focuses on various topics of empowerment. She also founded, Handmaidens in the Marketplace, a platform for women of faith who are ready to create a life they love that will enable them to better serve their family, church and community.